ONLY AMERICA'S #1 COIN GUIDE OFFERS NORMAN STACK'S AUTHORITATIVE TIPS:

- A clear photo of every U.S. coin—common or commemorative
- The four vital steps to correct coin identification
- Guaranteed dealer prices for every coin as valued in this guide
- A glossary of coin terms, information on mint marks and coin care, a cornucopia of collector's lore, and much, much more.

NORMAN STACK, senior partner in Stack's, the oldest, largest, and most renowned coin dealership in the United States, is a member of the International Association of Professional Numismatists. He is recognized as one of the world's foremost authorities in his field.

U.S. COINS OF VALUE 1982

Norman Stack

A DELL BOOK

Published by
Dell Publishing Co., Inc.
1 Dag Hammarskjold Plaza
New York, New York 10017

ISBN: 0-440-19347-8

Printed in the United States of America
First printing—January 1982

CONTENTS

PREFACE

Coins are my business—and they should be your concern. Why? Because many thousands of coins, *in circulation today*, are worth more than their face value. Right now, one or more of these coins might be in your pocket or purse, your basement or attic. Without realizing it, you might spend a penny for which I would gladly pay $5, $15, $25, $100. You might buy a newspaper with a nickel worth $20; purchase a package of cigarettes with a quarter valued at $35, a dime worth $90. Very simply, coins should be your concern because many coins have—or will have in the future—premium value.

The purpose of this book is to help you recognize three specific categories of coins: (1) coins that already have great to substantial premium value; (2) coins that already have modest to moderate premium value; (3) coins most likely to increase in premium value in the future.

I've compiled this book because buying and selling coins is my business. [*Editor's note:* Norman Stack is a partner in Stack's, America's oldest and largest coin dealership, in business for generations.] It is my hope that you and your friends and relatives will turn up coins that Stack's can purchase for its stock. The prices in this book are the prices we will gladly pay for the coins we need, in the conditions listed. [*Editor's note:* see pages 25-26 for a further explanation.]

It is also my hope that the following chapters will help to clarify a situation that grows more muddled every year: how to assess *accurately* the worth of premium-value coins. Unfortunately, as the interest in coins has grown, so too has the number of books written by authors whose business is neither buying nor selling coins. For many years, so-called average prices paid for coins have appeared in book after book—prices that are often too low or too high, prices that often have little to do with reality. Unfortunately, too, few of these books have stressed sufficiently that the condition of a coin is an important—sometimes the *only*—factor in determining its worth.

As you search for coins of value, it is important to know the fundamentals of identifying and judging a coin. Otherwise, like a New Jersey taxi driver who came to Stack's, you may be mistaken about the worth of your coins. This man *thought* he had found a 1909-S penny—worth $15-$18. What he had actually found was a 1909-S V.D.B. penny—worth $160!

Why didn't he know which coin he had? Because, like a great many people, he'd failed to look for *all* of the coin's identifying marks.

Don't allow this kind of mistake to happen to you. It's true, the taxi driver left Stack's happier than when he walked in, but, more often, such a story has an *un*happy end: identifying or judging a coin incorrectly usually results in disappointment, not joy.

As you'll see, the search for premium-value coins is fun—a treasure hunt in which every member of your family can, and should, participate. Some of the coins listed herein aren't likely to turn up in everyday change (though, believe me, it *can* happen), but with diligence and patience you will find many others. They *are* in circulation—or forgotten in drawers, safe-deposit boxes, etc.; they *are* salable or likely to be salable as time passes.

Just one last word before you begin your hunt: I urge you to take careful note of *all* the information that follows. You need these facts to get full value from this book—and, far more important, from the coins you find.

Norman Stack

January, 1982
Stack's
123 West 57th Street
New York, N.Y. 10019

1

WHAT MAKES A COIN VALUABLE?

SCARCITY

Contrary to popular belief, a coin isn't necessarily valuable merely because it is old. Like the value of most things, a coin's worth is determined largely on the basis of supply and demand. For this reason, scarcity is the single most important factor affecting the value of any coin.

For example, consider two Indian Head cents, one dated 1865, the other dated 1877, both in what coin dealers term "Fine" condition. Currently, the 1877 cent is worth $130; the 1865 cent—though twelve years older—is worth $1.75. Why the great difference in value? Because in 1865, the U. S. Mint struck 35 million Indian Head cents, while in 1877 the total output of Indian Head cents was less than one million. An 1877 cent is far harder to find than an 1865 cent; thus, an 1877 cent is far more valuable.

A coin becomes scarce or rare for a variety of reasons. Like the 1877 Indian Head cent just referred to, a coin may be scarce simply because it was minted in a smaller quantity than other coins of the same type. In some cases, a coin may have become scarce because its type was minted for only a few years (for example, the Flying Eagle cent) in other cases, even though a large quantity of a coin was minted, only relatively few still exist (for example, many Commemorative and gold coins). Occasionally, an overdate occurs (one numeral of the date superimposed over another). They are generally struck in small quantities and are therefore quite scarce. For example: the "1942" over "1" dime.

CONDITION

Perhaps because all of us handle coins every day of our lives, we are prone to forget that a coin is a tiny work of art. Designed by outstanding artists of the day, painstakingly produced, brilliant, lustrous coins are indeed objects of beauty.

It is for this reason that the condition of a coin is such an important factor in determining its worth. Just as an original Chippendale chair is worth more in fine condition than in poor condition, a premium-value coin is worth more in new condition than in worn condition. Thus, scarcity and condition are often equally important factors in determining the value of a coin. For example, a 1921-S Lincoln cent is worth $2.00 in "Very Fine" condition, but only 75¢ in "Very Good" condition. Here is a case—and there are many others—where a coin of a particular type and date is scarce *only* in choice condition. As you will note in reading this book, the prices listed for premium-value coins vary according to the coin's condition. Following are the terms and criteria used by dealers everywhere in grading condition.

Proof: The "deluxe" condition of a coin. Proof coins are struck from scientifically polished dies and blanks. A proof coin is free of imperfections, shines brilliantly like a mirror, with lettering and design full and sharp. It is an exquisite example of the art of coinage. Proof coins are not put into general circulation by the government. They are struck only for collectors and sold at more than face value. A proof *set* consists of a proof-condition cent, nickel, dime, quarter, and half dollar, struck in the same year.

Uncirculated: A coin in Uncirculated condition is exactly that—uncirculated, new and brilliant, showing no signs of wear or damage. Your bank receives uncirculated coins from the government's Federal Reserve System; you can often get uncirculated coins of the current year from your bank.

Extra (or) *Extremely Fine:* Coins in this condition have been in circulation just briefly, show only the slightest signs of wear and loss of luster. All details of design and lettering are as sharp as those on uncirculated coins. Generally, the 1973 and 1974 coins in your pocket or purse are likely to be in Extremely Fine condition.

Very Fine: A coin in Very Fine condition has usually been in circulation a year or two, shows some signs of wear, but all details of design and lettering are still sharp and bold.

Fine: Coins in Fine condition show obvious signs of circulation, but are worn only on the high points. The lettering and design are still sharp, but the details of both are not entirely visible.

Very Good and Good: Coins in these conditions have had considerable circulation and show it. They are worn in many spots, but most parts of the design and lettering are clear. Many of the details have been lost. "Very Good" describes a coin in better condition than "Good," but more worn than "Fine."

[*Editor's Note:* In this book, specific condition information precedes the listing for each type of coin except Commemorative issues.]

Scratches, dents and areas of pitting reduce the value of a coin in any given condition; however these flaws do not necessarily make a coin worthless. In large part, how much a flaw affects a coin's value depends on its scarcity.

Any coin that you hope to sell should be cared for carefully, and handled as little as possible. Always pick up a coin—even a worn coin—by its rim, *not* with your fingers across its surface. NEVER CLEAN YOUR COINS. If you do, you may give them an unnatural look and destroy their value. Most dealers refuse to purchase a coin that appears to have been cleaned; therefore, I repeat—because I know the temptation is great—DO NOT CLEAN YOUR COINS!

The best way to preserve coins you hope to sell in the future is to place each coin in a specially treated transparent envelope. These envelopes are available at most coin dealers and offer inexpensive protection from dust, moisture, and wear.

No matter how well-protected, all silver coins (even in Proof or Uncirculated condition) will tarnish a bit in time. Forestall this tarnishing process by using the envelopes just described, but if tarnishing does begin, do *not* use tarnish removers or other coin cleaners. Again, DO NOT CLEAN YOUR COINS. Restoration is risky, tricky work, requiring an expert's hand. Try it yourself, and you may reduce or destroy the value of a choice coin.

DEMAND

Like the value of paintings and sculpture, antiques and common stocks, the worth of premium-value coins fluctuates according to public demand—a demand that is sometimes fickle, even irrational. Generally, any fairly scarce coin in choice condition has premium value. Specifically, the *degree* of premium value is determined entirely by public demand. For example, consider these three premium-value coins: a 1931-S Lincoln cent; a 1927-S Liberty Standing quarter; an 1893 Liberty Head silver dollar. There were 866,000 1931-S Lincoln cents minted, and today the value of one of these cents in Very Fine condition is $18. There were 396,000 1927-S Liberty Standing quarters minted, and today one of these quarters in Fine condition is worth $5. There were 378,792 1893 Liberty Head silver dollars minted, and today one of these dollars in Extra Fine condition is worth $10. In other words, though the 1927-S Liberty Standing quarter and the 1893 Liberty Head silver dollar were minted in lesser quantities and are older coins, the 1931-S cent has increased far more in value. Why? Because as noted earlier, the degree of a coin's premium value is determined by public demand. Lincoln cents are extremely popular among collectors; thus, scarce or rare Lincoln cents have greater premium value than many other scarce or rare types of coins.

As you read through the listings in this book you will note many such seemingly "inconsistent" variations in the prices of premium-value coins. Bear in mind always that a coin's worth is determined by public demand; that, when a coin's value appears disproportionately high or low, the value is based upon the number of collectors who seek that specific coin.

To sum up, a coin's premium value is based on three (often interrelated) factors: scarcity, condition, demand. The prices listed in this book are, of course, based on these same three factors.

2

IDENTIFYING YOUR COINS CORRECTLY

Nothing makes a coin dealer happier than to be able to purchase a premium-value coin. (If you doubt that, bring your premium-value coins to Stack's and see how eager we are to buy.) Conversely, nothing makes a dealer *un*happier than to have to refuse to purchase a coin—to have to tell a would-be seller that he has identified his coin incorrectly, that the coin has little or no premium value. Unfortunately, the latter happening occurs all too often. For example, at Stack's it is a rare day when we don't encounter at least a dozen cases of "mistaken identity," coins brought or mailed to us that are *not*—as their owners believe—of premium value.

A difference in a mint mark, in the size of the stars, in a detail of the design—these are just three of many variations that may make one coin of a type different (and therefore more or less valuable) from other coins of the same type.

To make money from the sale of premium-value coins, you, of course, must be able to identify a coin of premium value. Otherwise, you'll waste time and effort (and, in most cases, be disappointed) by collecting coins that have little or no premium or potential premium value. It isn't possible for this, or any other book, to illustrate *every* variation of *every* type coin, but it is my hope that the text and photos that follow will help you to understand the process of identifying a coin correctly: what to look for, how certain kinds of variations appear, and more.

TYPE

Begin to establish a coin's correct identity by determining its type. In most cases, this determination is simple—either because the design on two coins of the same denomination is distinctly different (for example, no one could confuse a Lincoln-type cent with an Indian Head-type cent), and/or because the date on a coin is usually an accurate guide to pinpointing its type. In a few cases, however, determining a coin's type demands a careful eye. For example, consider the following three coins, all Large cents, all struck in the year 1793.

Chain Type

Wreath Type

Liberty Cap Type

The first cent is called a "Chain" type because the words "One Cent" on the reverse are surrounded by a design in the form of a chain. The second cent is called a "Wreath" type because the words "One Cent" on the reverse are surrounded by a design in the form of a wreath. The obverse sides of the Chain- and Wreath-type Large cents are similar enough to make identification difficult, but the reverse sides establish clearly which coin is which type. Now consider the third cent, a Liberty Cap type. The reverse of this coin is nearly identical to the reverse of the Wreath-type Large cent; thus, in this instance, it is a marked difference in the design of the obverse of the coins that distinguishes one type from the other.

As noted before, it isn't often that identifying a coin's type requires more than a flick of the eye. However, as the preceding example shows, the U. S. Mint has occasionally issued more than one type of coin of the same denomination in the same year. It is to your advantage to know how to determine coin types; it is to your advantage to know all you can about the many factors that distinguish one coin from another.

MINT MARKS

A mint mark (or the *absence* of a mint mark) on a coin tells at which U.S. Mint the coin was struck. The main U.S. Mint is in Philadelphia, Pennsylvania. At this time the government operates two branch mints—in Denver, Colorado and San Francisco, California—but at other times, branch mints have existed in these cities: New Orleans, Louisiana; Charlotte, North Carolina; Carson City, Nevada; Dahlonega, Georgia.

Coins struck at the Philadelphia Mint *do not* bear a mint mark; coins struck at a branch mint *do* carry a mint mark—a capital initial which designates the specific branch. Following are the mint marks (initials) that are (or have been) used to designate the various U. S. branch mints:

D	Denver, Colorado
D	Dahlonega, Georgia (gold coins only)
C	Charlotte, North Carolina (gold coins only)
O	New Orleans, Louisiana
CC	Carson City, Nevada
S	San Francisco, California

Note: From 1942–45, silver-content Jefferson nickels struck at the Philadelphia Mint bore the mint mark "P." No other coins struck at the Philadelphia Mint bear a mint mark.

Because a mint mark is often a factor affecting a coin's worth, it is important to look for this mark, to know what its presence—or absence—means. Consider three Liberty Standing quarters, all in Fine condition, all struck in the year 1919. The premium value of these coins depends entirely upon which mint they were struck. For example, with no mint mark (meaning the coin was struck in Philadelphia), one of these quarters is currently worth $5; with an "S" (San Francisco) mint mark, or with a "D" (Denver) mint mark, one of these quarters is currently worth $25.

Generally, a mint mark appears on the reverse of a coin; however, as this isn't always true, and as the placement of marks varies considerably, specific mint mark locations are listed under every type of coin within this book. To help you further, on the following pages are enlarged photos showing the position of the mint mark on various types of coins.

Indian Head Cent:
mint mark on reverse, at bottom, below wreath

Lincoln Cent:
mint mark on obverse, beneath date

Buffalo Nickel:
mint mark on reverse, below value

Jefferson Nickel (silver) 1942–45: mint mark on reverse, above dome

Jefferson Nickel (1938–64):
mint mark on reverse, to right of building

Liberty Seated Dime:
mint mark on reverse, within (shown) or below wreath

Liberty Head Dime:
mint mark on reverse,
at bottom, below wreath

Mercury Dime:
mint mark on reverse,
lower left of fasces

Roosevelt Dime (1946–64):
mint mark on reverse,
lower left of torch

Twenty-Cent Piece:
mint mark on reverse
below eagle

Liberty Seated Quarter:
mint mark on reverse,
below eagle

Liberty Head Quarter:
mint mark on reverse,
below eagle

Liberty Standing Quarter: mint mark on obverse, left, slightly above date

Washington Quarter (1932-64): mint mark on reverse, below eagle

Liberty Seated Half Dollar: mint mark on reverse, below eagle

Liberty Head Half Dollar: mint mark on reverse, below eagle

Liberty Walking Half Dollar: 1916–17, mint mark on obverse, below motto

Liberty Walking Half Dollar: 1917–47, mint mark on reverse, left of word HALF

Franklin Half Dollar: mint mark on reverse, above Liberty Bell beam

Liberty Seated Dollar: mint mark on reverse, below eagle

Liberty Head Dollar: mint mark on reverse, below eagle

Peace Dollar: mint mark on reverse, bottom, left of eagle's wing

EDGES

The design of a coin's edge (rim) is still another guide of identifying a coin correctly. Below are photos of the three most common edges in U. S. coinage.

Reeded Edge

Plain Edge

Lettered Edge

DIE VARIATIONS

As noted before, no one book can attempt to discuss or show all or even most die variations in U. S. coinage. (For example, there are 59 different varieties of the 1794 Liberty Cap Large cent alone.) However, because certain die variations are better known and/or more important than others, they are illustrated and discussed below. It is hoped that these examples will help you identify other die variations of the same kind (for example, other overdates) as well as to recognize the specific variations shown.

1864 Bronze Indian Head Cent with "L"

The designer's initial "L" appears on the obverse, on the ribbon. Because the initial is very small, it is clear only on Fine to Uncirculated specimens of the coin

The designer's initials "VDB" appear on the reverse, at the bottom between wheat stalks

Overdate:
Mercury Dime, "1942" over "1" Note: the numeral "2" is superimposed over the numeral "1"

Overdate:
Liberty Standing Quarter, "1918" over "7" Note: the numeral "8" is superimposed over the numeral "7"

1960 Lincoln Cent, Large and Small Date

1864 Two-Cent Bronze, Large and Small Motto

large motto

small motto

1955 Lincoln Cent

double die obverse

3

SAVING AND SELLING YOUR COINS

Basically, there are two kinds of coins that should interest those who hope to convert pennies into dollars: coins that already have substantial premium value; coins that are likely to have substantial premium value in the future.

As you perhaps know from experience, it is the latter group of coins that frequently causes confusion, disappointment, even anger among people who follow coin values. For it is this latter group which is difficult, often impossible, to sell. For example, *all* books that list coin values quote a current market price of 20¢-30¢ for a 1931 Lincoln cent in Very Good condition. But have you tried recently to sell such a coin to a dealer?

If you have, chances are the dealer refused the opportunity to buy your coin. Chances are, he explained, that, though this coin *does* have a modest premium value, his supply is plentiful and at this time he isn't buying more.

Currently, there are thousands of coins that, although worth more than face value, are *not* salable to a majority of professional dealers. Eventually, as years pass and the supply of these coins (in Choice condition) grows less plentiful, they *will* be sought after by dealers.

In my opinion, what you should do with these coins is save and preserve them (in the tarnish-resistant envelopes discussed in Chapter I). What you should also do is look for the best specimens of these coins—for example, if you have a 1931 Lincoln cent in Very Good condition, be on the lookout for the same type coin in Very Fine condition; then try to find a specimen in Extra Fine condition. In other words, try always to upgrade the condition of coins you're saving, with an eye toward the future. The better the condition of those coins, the more they'll be worth when coins of that type are in demand.

As you read through this book, you will note that an asterisk (*) appears next to many of the prices listed. That asterisk means two things: (1) in my opinion, that these are the coins most likely to increase in premium value in the future, and, (2) at the present time, Stack's is well supplied with these coins and will *not* (repeat, will *not*) be purchasing more in the near future.

In addition to coins marked with an asterisk, Stack's also reserves the right to set a limit on the number of coin sets submitted, or on the quantity of coins of any single denomination.

The time to begin looking for coins of value is now—today. Learn enough about familiar coins so that a coin of high premium value (for example, a 1955 Lincoln cent doubled die obverse) couldn't slip through your fingers unnoticed. Look for old coins your grandmother may have tucked away among her keepsakes; look through the drawers of old desks and chests stored in your attic or basement; look behind the cushion of a leather chair that has been in your family for years.

HOW TO SELL YOUR PREMIUM-VALUE COINS TO STACK'S

Stack's wants very much to purchase coins of premium value, *except* for those coins listed with an asterisk [*], and discussed on page 25. With the exception of gold coins (see below), the prices quoted in this book are the prices Stack's pays for coins we need, in the condition listed. More specifically, the prices listed herein are the *minimum* Stack's pays for coins we need, in the condition listed. We never pay less than a price quoted, and often—as many readers can attest—we pay more. Why? In most cases, because the owner of a coin has misjudged its condition. For example, you might send us a 1921 Mercury dime which you believe is in "Good" condition and therefore worth $7.50. However, if Stack's finds that your dime is in "Fine" condition, you will receive $25—the price we pay for that coin in "Fine" condition.

Very simply, if you err in judging a coin's worth, Stack's won't take advantage of your willingness to accept the price listed herein. We are the oldest coin dealership in this country and we intend not only to remain in business but to retain our reputation. In short, even if you aren't fully aware of a coin's worth, we are—and we will pay for the coin accordingly.

If you can't bring your coins to Stack's, mail them, following this procedure: wrap each coin in paper; place the wrapped coins between two pieces of cardboard and tape together. (Note: do *not* tape coin[s] to cardboard; this can destroy a coin's value.) Write your name and address on a slip of paper; enclose this slip with your coins in an envelope. *Insure the coins*; mail them to

Stack's, 123 West 57th Street, New York, N.Y. 10019

I repeat: *Insure the package containing your coins, identify it clearly—inside and out—as belonging to you.*

If your coins are of the type and/or condition Stack's needs, we will gladly buy them. If they aren't, we will return your coins by insured mail.

The prices listed for "common" silver coins in this book are based largely on the price of silver: approximately $8 per ounce as this book goes to press. Should the price of silver increase or decrease, the price of these coins will increase or decrease accordingly.

The prices listed for "common" gold coins in this book are based largely on the price of gold; approximately $500 per ounce as this book goes to press. Should the price of gold increase or decrease, the price of these coins will increase or decrease accordingly.

4

A GLOSSARY OF COIN TERMS

ALTERED DATE: A fake date on a coin—a date altered unscrupulously to make a coin appear to be one of a rarer (thus more valuable) issue.

COMMEMORATIVE COIN: A coin issued to mark a special event or to honor an outstanding person or historical happening. Commemorative coins are not intended for general use, but are legal tender.

CONDITION: The appearance of a coin; its physical state. (See also Chapter 1.)

DESIGNER (sometimes called *Engraver*): The artist who creates a coin's design. Occasionally, one man designs a coin's obverse, another the reverse. Often, the designer(s)'s initials appear on the coin.

DIE: A piece of metal engraved with the design of the obverse or reverse of a coin. A die is used to impress the design on a flan (a metal blank cut to the shape of a coin).

DIE DEFECT: A defect in a coin caused by a defective die.

DIE VARIATION: Any major or minor alteration in the basic design of a coin.

DOUBLE DIE: A double image on a coin, the result of the die being struck (mistakenly) twice. (See photo, page 23.)

DOUBLE EAGLE: A $20 gold coin.

EAGLE: A $10 gold coin.

FACE VALUE: The denomination of a coin.

FLAN (also called *Planchet*): A blank piece of metal in the size and shape of a coin.

FRACTIONAL CURRENCY: Certain paper notes issued by the United States Government from 1862 to 1876 to relieve the shortage of minor coins. They ranged from three cents to fifty cents in value.

HALF EAGLE: A $5 gold coin.

INCUSE COIN: A coin on which the design has been impressed below the coin's surface. (When the design is raised above the coin's surface, the coin is said to be in *relief*.)

LEGEND (sometimes called *Inscription*): On current U.S. coins, the words "United States of America."

LETTERED EDGE: Lettering that runs around a coin's rim. (See photo, page 20).

MARKET VALUE: The price at which a dealer may buy a coin.

MILLED EDGE: The serration on a coin's rim.

MINT ERRORS: Mistakes or defects in coins produced by a government mint.

MINT MARK: A capital letter on a coin that indicates at which mint that coin was struck. (See photos, pages 17–20.) *Note:* Coins struck at the Philadelphia Mint do not have a mint mark, except nickels, 1942–45.

MIS-STRIKE: A mint error, resulting in a coin with an off-center design.

MOTTO: On current U. S. coins, these two phrases: "In God We Trust" and "E Pluribus Unum."

NUMISMATICS: The study and science of coins, tokens, medals, and paper money.

OBVERSE: The "heads" or "face" side of a coin; generally the side with the date and principal design.

OVERDATE: One date superimposed over another. (See photos, page 22.)

PATTERN COIN: A coin of a new denomination or with a new design or a partially new design that is not issued for general circulation; in short, an "experimental" coin.

PREMIUM VALUE: The price (above face value) at which a coin can be sold.

PROOF COINS: Coins struck by the U. S. Mint for collectors. These coins have a special brilliance, exceptionally sharp details, and no imperfections. (See also Chapter 1.)

PROOF SET: A set of coins Proof condition containing one cent, one nickel, one dime, one quarter, and one half dollar, struck in the same year. A proof set is packaged in a special container; now sold only by the San Francisco Mint.

QUARTER EAGLE: A $2.50 gold coin.

REEDED EDGE: A coin edge with grooved lines that run vertically around its perimeter. (See photo, page 20.)

RELIEF: Any part of a coin's design that is raised above the coin's surface is said to be in *relief*. The opposite of relief is *incuse*.

RESTRIKE: A coin struck from original dies later (usually several years) than the date on the coin.

REVERSE: The back or "tails" side of a coin.

ROLL: A standard number of coins from the same mint,

of the same denomination and year—usually in Uncirculated condition. According to denomination, the following number of coins are considered a "roll": 50 cents, 40 nickels, 50 dimes, 40 quarters, 20 half dollars.

SERIES COLLECTING: Collecting one coin of each year, issued from each mint, including important die variations, of a specific design and denomination. For example, collecting Lincoln cents from 1909 to the present. Many coin lovers are series collectors, trying always to fill in on missing dates, mint marks, etc.; trying too to find coins in better condition than those they already have.

TYPE: A coin's basic distinguishing design, which may appear on either the obverse or reverse. The majority of coins of the same type will have one or more die variations.

TYPE COLLECTING: Collecting coins of the same basic design, including all die variations. A type collector's object is to have one coin (in the best condition possible) of each variation issued of a specific type. For example, a type collector of the Lincoln cent would want to possess the four existing varieties of this coin type.

UNCIRCULATED: A term describing the condition of a coin that has never been circulated. (See also Chapter 1.)

5

HALF CENTS

Half-cent pieces were struck in copper from 1793 to 1857. They have the lowest face value of any coin issued in this country.

The half-cent piece has the distinction (along with the twenty-cent and three-dollar gold piece;) of being one of the most unpopular coins ever struck by the U. S. Mint for general circulation.

When the half cent was issued, copper coins were not legal tender in this country, so banks and shopkeepers usually refused to accept them as currency. This unpopularity naturally limited their circulation, and quantities of them often were accumulated by banks or by individuals. From time to time, large hoards of half-cent pieces have been found, usually in very good condition, making more of these coins available to collectors. This accounts for the comparatively moderate prices many half-cent pieces command, considering their early dates.

Designs of the half cents closely followed those of the large cent that appeared a few years before. The four basic types of half cents issued are: Liberty with Cap (1793–97); Liberty with Draped Bust (1800–08); Liberty with Turban (1809–36); and Liberty with Braided Hair (1849–57). Within these types, there are many variations.

LIBERTY WITH CAP

liberty facing left

CONDITION: *Good:* Liberty and wreath outlined but most details worn smooth; lettering and date readable. *Fine:* Most details of design visible; lettering and date sharp.

MINT MARK: None.

Date	*Good*	*Fine*	*Amount Minted*
1793	$635.00	$1,100.00	31,934

liberty facing right with pole to cap — *with no pole to cap*

Date	*Good*	*Fine*	*Amount Minted*
1794	$ 125.00	$ 235.00	81,600
1795	95.00	170.00	25,600
1796 with pole to cap	1,275.00	2,300.00	115,480
1796 with no pole to cap	1,925.00	3,850.00	
1797	95.00	160.00	107,048
1797 with lettered edge	325.00	500.00	

LIBERTY WITH DRAPED BUST

CONDITION: *Good:* Liberty and wreath outlined but most details worn smooth; lettering and date readable. *Fine:* Most details of hair and drapery worn; most other details visible; lettering and date sharp.

MINT MARK: None.

Date	*Good*	*Fine*	*Amount Minted*
1800	$ 16.50	$ 27.50	211,530
1802	160.00	275.00	14,366
1803	14.00	20.00	97,900
1804	14.00	18.00	1,055,312
1805	14.00	18.00	814,464
1806	14.00	18.00	356,000
1807	14.00	18.00	476,000
1808	14.00	18.00	400,000
1808 with 08 over 07	40.00	80.00	

LIBERTY WITH TURBAN

CONDITION: *Good:* Liberty and wreath outlined but most details worn smooth; word LIBERTY on headband partly visible; other lettering and date readable. *Fine:* Most details of design and word LIBERTY on headband visible; other lettering and date sharp. *Proof:* Coin should be in unused condition.

MINT MARK: None.

Date	*Good*	*Fine*	*Amount Minted*
1809	$12.50	$15.00	1,154,572
1809 with 9 over 6	12.50	20.00	
1809 with circle in 0	12.50	20.00	
1810	12.50	15.00	215,000
1811	45.00	95.00	63,140
1825	12.50	15.00	63,000
1826	12.50	15.00	234,000
1828	12.50	15.00	606,000
1829	12.50	15.00	487,000
1832	12.50	15.00	154,000
1833	12.50	15.00	154,000
1834	12.50	15.00	154,000
1835	12.50	15.00	141,000
1837 token	12.50	30.00	——

	Proof	
1831 Original (large berries on wreath)	$1,750.00	——
1831 Restrike (small berries on wreath)	1,500.00	——
1836 Original (large berries on wreath)	1,600.00	398,000
1836 Restrike (small berries on wreath)	1,500.00	

LIBERTY WITH BRAIDED HAIR

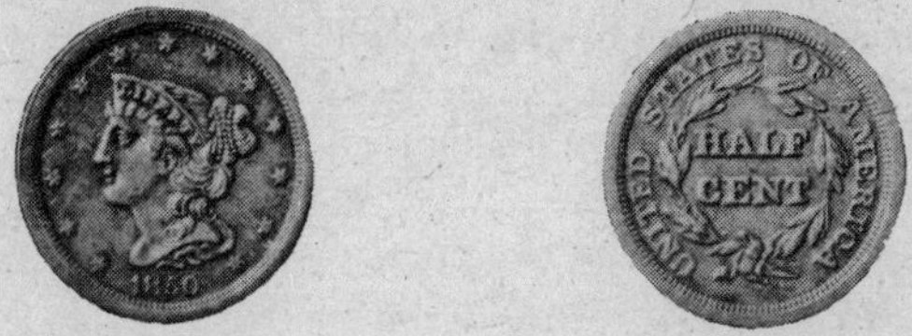

CONDITION: *Good:* Liberty and wreath outlined but most details worn smooth; word LIBERTY on crown worn but readable, other lettering and date readable. *Fine:* Some details of hair worn, beads on hair cords and other details of design visible; lettering and date sharp. *Proof:* Coin should be in unused condition.

MINT MARK: None.

Date	*Good*	*Fine*	*Amount Minted*
1849	$17.50	$25.00	39,864
1850	15.00	20.00	39,812
1851	15.00	20.00	147,672
1853	15.00	20.00	129,694
1854	15.00	20.00	55,358
1855	15.00	20.00	56,500
1856	15.00	20.00	40,430
1857	22.50	27.50	35,180

	Proof	
1840 Original (large berries on wreath)	$1,425.00	——
1840 Restrike (small berries on wreath)	1,375.00	——
1841 Original (large berries on wreath)	1,425.00	——
1841 Restrike (small berries on wreath)	1,325.00	——
1842 Original (large berries on wreath)	1,425.00	——

1842 Restrike (small berries on wreath)	$1,375.00	———
1843 Original (large berries on wreath)	1,425.00	———
1843 Restrike (small berries on wreath)	1,375.00	———
1844 Original (large berries on wreath)	1,550.00	———
1844 Restrike (small berries on wreath)	1,425.00	———
1845 Original (large berries on wreath)	1,425.00	———
1845 Restrike (small berries on wreath)	1,425.00	———
1846 Original (large berries on wreath)	1,550.00	———
1846 Restrike (small berries on wreath)	1,375.00	———
1847 Original (large berries on wreath)	1,425.00	———
1847 Restrike (small berries on wreath)	1,425.00	———
1848 Original (large berries on wreath)	1,375.00	———
1848 Restrike (small berries on wreath)	1,375.00	———
1849 Original (large berries on wreath)	1,375.00	———
1849 Restrike (small berries on wreath)	1,200.00	———
1852 Original (large berries on wreath)	7,000.00	———
1852 Restrike (small berries on wreath)	1,200.00	———

6

LARGE CENTS

Large cents were struck in copper from 1793 to 1857. Like the half-cent piece, this large copper coin was not legal tender at the time of its issue. It did not, however, suffer the extreme unpopularity of the half cent.

Large cents are among the most interesting series of U.S. coins, because so many variations were produced during single-year issues. In 1794 alone there were 59 variations of the same design. This was primarily due to the lack of a master die before 1817. (Because of the Mint fire in 1816, new, improved machinery was installed, so that coinage became more mechanized and the number of variations dropped sharply.)

Gradually, large cents started to become a problem for both the government and the public. For the people, the large coin proved too clumsy to handle. For the government the coin proved too costly to issue, because of the rising price of copper. It had reached the point where the government was losing money on every cent minted. Both problems were successfully solved by discontinuing the large cent and introducing the small cent in its place (see page 44).

There were seven basic types of large cents issued: Liberty, Chain Type (1793); Liberty, Wreath Type (1793); Liberty with Cap (1793–96); Liberty with Draped Bust

(1796–1807); Liberty with Turban (1808–14); Liberty with Coronet (1816–39); Liberty with Braided Hair (1839–57).

LIBERTY, CHAIN TYPE

with AMERICA

with AMERI.

CONDITION: *Good:* Liberty and chain outlined but most details worn smooth; lettering and date worn but readable. *Fine:* Most details of hair and all links in chain visible; lettering and date sharp.

MINT MARK: None.

Date	*Good*	*Fine*	*Amount Minted*
1793 with AMERICA	$500.00	$1,250.00	112,212
1793 with AMERI.	550.00	1,325.00	

LIBERTY, WREATH TYPE

CONDITION: *Good:* Liberty and wreath outlined but most details worn smooth; lettering and date readable. *Fine:* Most details of hair and wreath visible; lettering and date sharp.

MINT MARK: None.

Date	*Good*	*Fine*	*Amount Minted*
1793	$400.00	$900.00	101,156

LIBERTY WITH CAP

CONDITION: *Good:* Liberty and wreath outlined but most details worn; lettering and date readable. *Fine:* Most details of hair visible; lettering and date sharp.

MINT MARK: None.

Date	*Good*	*Fine*	*Amount Minted*
1793	$450.00	$1,200.00	11,056
1794	32.50	62.50	918,521
1795	27.50	50.00	82,000
1795 with lettered edge	37.50	105.00	
1796	35.00	85.00	974,700

LIBERTY WITH DRAPED BUST

CONDITION: *Good:* Liberty outlined but most details worn smooth; lettering and date worn but readable. *Fine:* Hair at forehead and some drapery details worn; other details visible; lettering and date sharp.

MINT MARK: None.

Date	*Good*	*Fine*	*Amount Minted*
1796	$ 25.00	$ 57.50	included above
1797	9.50	25.00	897,510
1797 with stemless wreath	32.50	95.00	
1798	8.50	19.00	979,700
1798 with 8 over 7	18.50	55.00	
1799	360.00	575.00	904,585
1799 with 99 over 98	385.00	715.00	

1800	7.50	20.00	2,822,175
1801	8.50	20.00	1,362,837
1802	6.50	16.50	3,435,100
1803	6.50	16.50	2,471,353
1804	185.00	400.00	756,838
1805	7.50	17.50	941,116
1806	20.00	57.50	348,000
1807	6.50	16.50	727,221

LIBERTY WITH TURBAN

CONDITION: *Good:* Liberty and wreath outlined but most details worn smooth; word LIBERTY on headband partly worn; other lettering and date readable: *Fine:* Details of hair at forehead and ear worn; other details, all lettering, and date sharp.

MINT MARK: None.

Date	*Good*	*Fine*	*Amount Minted*
1808	$ 9.50	$27.50	1,109,000
1809	40.00	95.00	222,867
1810	9.00	25.00	1,485,500
1811	17.50	50.00	218,025
1812	9.00	25.00	1,075,500
1813	10.00	35.00	418,000
1814	9.00	25.00	357,830

LIBERTY WITH CORONET

CONDITION: *Good:* Liberty and wreath outlined but most details worn smooth; most lettering and date readable. *Fine:* Some hair details worn; other details, including cords on hair, visible; lettering and date sharp.

MINT MARK: None.

Date	*Good*	*Fine*	*Amount Minted*
1816	$ 3.50	$ 6.00	2,820,982
1817	3.50	6.00	3,948,400
1818	3.50	6.00	3,167,000
1819	3.50	6.00	2,671,000
1820	3.50	6.00	4,407,550
1821	7.50	25.00	389,000
1822	3.50	6.00	2,072,339
1823	14.50	35.00	855,730
1824	3.50	6.00	1,262,000
1825	3.50	6.00	1,461,100
1826	3.50	6.00	1,517,425
1827	3.50	6.00	2,357,732
1828	3.50	6.00	2,260,624
1829	3.50	6.00	1,414,500
1830	3.50	6.00	1,711,500
1831	3.50	6.00	3,359,260
1832	3.50	6.00	2,362,000
1833	3.50	6.00	2,739,000
1834	3.50	6.00	1,855,100
1835	3.50	6.00	3,878,400
1836	3.50	6.00	2,111,000
1837	3.50	6.00	5,558,300
1838	3.50	6.00	6,370,200

LIBERTY WITH BRAIDED HAIR

CONDITION: *Good:* Liberty and wreath outlined but most details worn smooth; word LIBERTY on crown, other lettering, and date readable. *Fine:* Most details of hair and beads on hair cords visible; lettering and date sharp.

MINT MARK: None.

Date	*Good*	*Fine*	*Amount Minted*
1839	$ 3.50	$ 7.00	3,128,661
1839 with 9 over 6	60.00	135.00	
1840	3.50	5.00	2,462,700
1841	5.00	7.50	1,597,367
1842	3.50	5.00	2,383,390
1843	3.50	5.00	2,428,320
1844	3.50	5.00	2,398,752
1845	3.50	5.00	3,894,804
1846	3.50	5.00	4,120,800
1847	3.50	5.00	6,183,669
1848	3.50	5.00	6,415,799
1849	3.50	5.00	4,178,500
1850	3.50	5.00	4,426,844
1851	3.50	5.00	9,889,707
1852	3.50	5.00	5,063,094
1853	3.50	5.00	6,641,131
1854	3.50	5.00	4,236,156
1855	3.50	5.00	1,574,829
1856	3.50	5.00	2,690,463
1857	9.50	17.00	333,456

7

SMALL CENTS

Small cents were first struck in 1856. With their new small size and new composition, they were the answer to the problems posed by the large cent.

The first small cent issued was the Flying Eagle cent. The new material for it was composed of 88 parts copper to 12 parts nickel, giving the coin a whitish appearance. The obverse of this handsome coin, designed by J. B. Longacre, was influenced by the reverse of the Gobrecht silver dollar. Since the Flying Eagle cent was not formally authorized until 1857, the 1856 issue is generally considered a pattern coin.

In 1859, the Flying Eagle cent was replaced by the Indian Head cent, also designed by J. B. Longacre. This was —and still is among collectors—one of the most popular coins ever issued. The material used remained unchanged until 1864, when the price of nickel increased. The composition was then changed to bronze—95 parts copper to 5 parts tin and zinc.

In 1909, on the centennial of Abraham Lincoln's birthday, the Indian Head cent was replaced by the Lincoln cent, another extremely popular coin, which is still being issued. Two major changes took place in the minting of this coin.

The first change occurred during World War II, when

the composition of the coin was changed from bronze to steel, with a light coat of zinc. This change was necessary due to the wartime shortage of copper. However, the new composition proved unsatisfactory because these cents were often mistaken for dimes. In 1946, the small cent returned to its prewar composition of bronze.

The other major change took place in 1959, when the wreath on the reverse of the Lincoln cent was discontinued and replaced by a design of the Lincoln Memorial at Washington, D.C. This change was made in commemoration of the sesquicentennial of Lincoln's birth.

FLYING EAGLE CENT

CONDITION: *Good:* Eagle and wreath clearly outlined but most details worn; lettering and date clear. *Fine:* All details of design visible; lettering and date sharp.

MINT MARK: None.

Date	*Good*	*Fine*	*Amount Minted*
1856	$650.00	$875.00	———
1857	4.00	7.00	17,450,000
1858 with large letters	4.00	7.00	24,600,000
1858 with small letters	4.00	7.00	

INDIAN HEAD CENT

without shield *with shield*

CONDITION: *Good:* Indian Head and wreath outlined, but most details of feathers worn; lettering and date readable. *Fine:* Some feather details visible; other details, word LIBERTY on headband, other lettering sharp.

MINT MARK: On reverse, under wreath.

Date	*Good*	*Fine*	*Amount Minted*
1859 without shield	$ 1.10	$ 3.25	36,400,000
1860	1.10	2.25	20,566,000
1861	2.25	5.00	10,100,000
1862	1.10	1.75	28,075,000
1863	1.10	1.75	49,840,000
1864 copper-nickel	1.75	3.25	13,740,000
1864 bronze	1.00	2.25	39,233,714
1864 bronze-"L" on ribbon	10.00	22.50	
1865	1.00	1.75	35,429,286
1866	5.50	11.00	9,826,500
1867	5.50	11.00	9,821,000
1868	5.00	11.00	10,266,500
1869	8.50	15.50	6,420,000
1870	7.00	11.00	5,275,000
1871	11.00	16.00	3,929,500
1872	11.00	19.00	4,042,000
1873	2.00	4.75	11,676,500
1874	2.00	4.75	14,187,500
1875	2.00	4.75	13,528,000

1876	2.50	6.00	7,944,000
1877	90.00	130.00	852,500
1878	3.00	6.00	5,799,850
1879	.65*	1.75	16,231,200
1880	.40*	.90*	38,964,955
1881	.45*	.95*	39,211,575
1882	.45*	.95*	38,581,100
1883	.45*	.95*	45,598,109
1884	.70*	1.50	23,261,742
1885	1.00	3.25	11,765,384
1886	.75*	1.50	17,654,290
1887	.30*	.50*	45,226,483
1888	.30*	.50*	37,494,414
1889	.30*	.50*	48,869,361
1890	.30*	.50*	57,182,854
1891	.30*	.50*	47,072,350
1892	.30*	.50*	37,649,832
1893	.30*	.50*	46,642,195
1894	.30*	1.00	16,752,132
1895	.30*	.50*	38,343,636
1896	.30*	.50*	39,057,293
1897	.30*	.50*	50,466,330
1898	.30*	.50*	49,823,079
1899	.30*	.50*	53,600,031
1900	.30*	.50*	66,833,764
1901	.30*	.50*	79,611,143
1902	.30*	.50*	87,376,722
1903	.30*	.50*	85,094,493
1904	.30*	.50*	61,328,015
1905	.30*	.50*	80,719,163
1906	.30*	.50*	96,022,255
1907	.30*	.50*	108,138,618
1908	.30*	.50*	32,327,987
1908-S	8.00	9.00	1,115,000
1909	.30*	.50*	14,370,645
1909-S	35.00	50.00	309,000

** Coins marked with an asterisk are discussed on pages 25-26.*

LINCOLN CENT

with wheat

with memorial

CONDITION: *V. Good:* Most details of wheat stalks and Lincoln head visible; lettering and date sharp. *V. Fine:* All details of design, lettering, and date sharp.

MINT MARK: On obverse, below the date.

Date	*V. Good*	*V. Fine*	*Amount Minted*
1909	$ .05*	$ .20*	72,702,618
1909 V.D.B.	.50*	.75*	27,995,000
1909-S	15.00	18.00	1,825,000
1909-S V.D.B.	120.00	160.00	484,000
1910	.05*	.20*	146,801,218
1910-S	3.00	4.00	6,045,000
1911	.05*	.35*	101,177,787
1911-D	1.00	1.75	12,672,000
1911-S	4.50	6.00	4,026,000
1912	.05*	.20*	68,153,060
1912-D	1.00	1.50	10,411,000
1912-S	3.50	4.50	4.431,000
1913	.05*	.35*	76,532,352
1913-D	.25*	1.25	15,804,000
1913-S	2.00	2.50	6,101,000
1914	.20*	.75*	75,238,432
1914-D	25.00	60.00	1,193,000
1914-S	3.50	4.00	4,137,000
1915	.50*	.80*	29,092,120
1915-D	.20*	.75*	22,050,000
1915-S	2.00	2.50	4,833,000
1916	.05*	.35*	131,833,677
1916-D	.20*	.80*	35,956,000

** Coins marked with an asterisk are discussed on pages 25-26.*

1916-S	.20*	.80*	22,510,000
1917	.05*	.40*	196,429,785
1917 D	.20*	.50*	55,120,000
1917-S	.20*	.50*	32,620,000
1918	.01	.40*	288,104,634
1918-D	.20*	.50*	47,830,000
1918-S	.20*	.50*	34,680,000
1919	.01	.40*	392,021,000
1919-D	.20*	.50*	57,154,000
1919-S	.20*	.50*	139,760,000
1920	.20*	.40*	310,165,000
1920-D	.20*	.55*	49,280,000
1920-S	.20*	.55*	46,220,000
1921	.20*	.50*	39,157,000
1921-S	.75*	2.00	15,274,000
1922-D	2.00	2.50	
1922 Denver Mint			7,160,000
(without D)	20.00	35.00	
1923	.01	.15*	74,723,000
1923-S	.55*	5.00	8,700,000
1924	.01	.35*	75,178,000
1924-D	4.50	7.00	2,520,000
1924-S	.45*	2.50	11,696,000
1925	.01	.15*	139,949,000
1925-D	.20*	.45*	22,580,000
1925-S	.20*	.45*	26,380,000
1926	.01	.15*	157,088,000
1926-D	.20*	.40*	28,020,000
1926-S	1.00	1.50	4,550,000
1927	.01	.15*	144,440,000
1927-D	.20*	.50*	27,170,000
1927-S	.45*	.80*	14,276,000
1928	.01	.05*	134,116,000
1928-D	.05*	.35*	31,170,000
1928-S	.20*	.40*	17,266,000
1929	.01	.05*	185,622,000
1929-D	.01	.15*	41,730,000
1929-S	.01	.15*	50,148,000
1930	.01	.15*	157,415,000

** Coins marked with an asterisk are discussed on pages 25-26.*

1930-D	.01	.05*	40,100,000
1930-S	.01	.05*	24,286,000
1931	.20*	.30*	19,396,000
1931-D	1.00	1.50	4,480,000
1931-S	15.00	18.00	866,000
1932	.20*	.45*	9,062,000
1932-D	.20*	.55*	10,500,000
1933	.20*	.55*	14,360,000
1933-D	.55*	.70*	6,200,000
1934	.01	.01	219,080,000
1934-D	.01	.01	28,446,000
1935	.01	.01	245,388,000
1935-D	.01	.01	47,000,000
1935-S	.01	.01	38,702,000
1936	.01	.01	309,637,569
1936-D	.01	.01	40,620,000
1936-S	.01	.01	29,130,000
1937	.01	.01	309,179,320
1937-D	.01	.01	50,430,000
1937-S	.01	.01	34,500,000
1938	.01	.01	156,696,734
1938-D	.01	.01	20,010,000
1938-S	.01	.01	15,180,000
1939	.01	.01	316,479,520
1939-D	.10*	.25*	15,160,000
1939-S	.01	.01	52,070,000
1940	.01	.01	586,825,872
1940-D	.01	.01	81,390,000
1940-S	.01	.01	112,940,000
1941	.01	.01	887,039,100
1941-D	.01	.01	128,700,000
1941-S	.01	.01	92,360,000
1942	.01	.01	657,828,600
1942-D	.01	.01	206,698,000
1942-S	.01	.01	85,590,000
1943 steel	.01	.01	684,628,670
1943-D steel	.01	.01	217,660,000
1943-S steel	.01	.01	191,550,000
1944	.01	.01	1,435,400,000

** Coins marked with an asterisk are discussed on pages 25-26.*

1944-D	.01	.01	430,578,000
1944-S	.01	.01	282,760,000
1945	.01	.01	1,040,515,000
1945-D	.01	.01	226,268,000
1945-S	.01	.01	181,770,000
1946	.01	.01	991,655,000
1946-D	.01	.01	315,690,000
1946-S	.01	.01	198,100,000
1947	.01	.01	190,555,000
1947-D	.01	.01	194,750,000
1947-S	.01	.01	99,000,000
1948	.01	.01	317,570,000
1948-D	.01	.01	172,637,500
1948-S	.01	.01	81,735,000
1949	.01	.01	217,490,000
1949-D	.01	.01	154,370,500
1949-S	.01	.01	64,290,000
1950	.01	.01	272,686,386
1950-D	.01	.01	334,950,000
1950-S	.01	.01	118,505,000
1951	.01	.01	294,633,500
1951-D	.01	.01	625,355,000
1951-S	.01	.01	100,890,000
1952	.01	.01	186,856,980
1952-D	.01	.01	746,130,000
1952-S	.01	.01	137,800,004
1953	.01	.01	256,883,800
1953-D	.01	.01	700,515,000
1953-S	.01	.01	181,835,000
1954	.01	.01	71,873,350
1954-D	.01	.01	251,552,500
1954-S	.01	.01	96,190,000
1955	.01	.01	330,958,200
1955 double die obv. (see illus. p. 23)	85.00	125.00	
1955-D	.01	.01	563,257,500
1955-S	.05*	.10*	44,610,000
1956	.01	.01	421,414,384
1956-D	.01	.01	1,098,201,100

* *Coins marked with an asterisk are discussed on pages 25-26.*

1957	.01	.01	283,787,952
1957-D	.01	.01	1,051,342,000
1958	.01	.01	253,400,652
1958-D	.01	.01	800,953,300
1959	.01	.01	610,864,291
1959-D	.01	.01	1,279,760,000
1960 with large date	.01	.01	588,096,602
1960 with small date	.01	.60*	
1960-D with large date	.01	.01	1,580,884,000
1960-D with small date	.01	.01	
1961	.01	.01	756,373,244
1961-D	.01	.01	1,753,266,700
1962	.01	.01	609,263,019
1962-D	.01	.01	1,793,148,400
1963	.01	.01	754,110,000
1963-D	.01	.01	1,774,020,400
1964	.01	.01	2,652,525,762
1964-D	.01	.01	3,799,071,500
1965	.01	.01	2,058,579,000
1966	.01	.01	2,188,147,783
1967	.01	.01	3,048,667,100
1968	.01	.01	1,707,880,970
1968-D	.01	.01	2,886,269,600
1968-S	.01	.01	261,311,510
1969	.01	.01	1,136,910,000
1969-D	.01	.01	4,002,832,200
1969-S	.01	.01	547,309,631
1970	.01	.01	1,898,315,000
1970-D	.01	.01	2,891,438,900
1970-S	.01	.01	693,192,814
1971	.01	.01	1,919,490,000
1971-D	.01	.01	2,911,045,600
1971-S	.01	.01	528,354,192
1972	.01	.01	2,933,255,000
1972-D	.01	.01	2,665,071,400
1972-S	.01	.01	380,200,104
1973-1982	.01	.01	———

* *Coins marked with an asterisk are discussed on pages 25-26.*

8

TWO-CENT PIECE

This bronze coin, struck from 1864 through 1873, was issued to help alleviate the serious shortage of coins during the Civil War. This coin was authorized by Congress together with the bronze small cent of 1864.

The two-cent piece was the first U. S. coin to carry the now-familiar phrase IN GOD WE TRUST, a motto that reflects the religious sentiment that prevailed during the Civil War.

This coin was widely circulated during its first years of issue. But when there proved to be no real need for this denomination, the amount of two-cent pieces issued began to decrease each year. In its final year of issue, the coin was struck in proof only.

Only one type of two-cent piece was issued: the obverse shows a large shield, a design that was later adopted for use on the early five-cent piece.

CONDITION: *Good:* Shield outlined, but most details worn

smooth; most words of motto readable; other lettering and date worn but readable. *Fine:* Details of shield, wheat stalks, and full motto visible; other lettering and date sharp. *Proof:* Coin should be in unused condition.

MINT MARK: None.

Date	*Good*	*Fine*	*Amount Minted*
1864 with small motto	$22.50	$45.00	19,847,500
1864 with large motto	4.00	6.00	
1865	4.00	6.00	13,640,000
1866	4.00	6.00	3,177,000
1867	4.00	6.00	2,938,750
1868	4.00	6.00	2,803,750
1869	4.00	6.00	1,546,500
1870	4.00	6.00	861,250
1871	4.00	6.00	721,250
1872	25.00	50.00	65,000

	Proof	
1873	$1,200.00	600

9

THREE-CENT PIECES

Three-cent pieces were struck in silver, from 1851 to 1873, and in nickel, from 1865 to 1889.

The silver three-cent piece was issued at the same time the three-cent postage rate went into effect to facilitate the purchase of the three-cent stamp. This was the second smallest coin ever struck at the U. S. Mint (the early gold dollar was the smallest). While this silver coin was popular during its first year of issue, its small size made handling difficult and its popularity quickly waned. During its last 11 years of issue, the coin was struck in proof only. The obverse of the silver three-cent piece shows a six-pointed star; the reverse shows the value in Roman numerals, within a large C (for cents).

The nickel three-cent piece was issued to redeem fractional currency of that denomination, issued because of the coin shortage during the Civil War. The "nickel" was actually an alloy composed of nickel, copper and zinc. Although larger in size than its silver counterpart, this piece was not widely popular and the amount of coins minted slowly dwindled until the coin and the denomination were finally discontinued. The obverse of the nickel three-cent piece shows a Liberty head; the reverse shows the value in Roman numerals encircled by a wreath.

SILVER THREE-CENT PIECE

CONDITION: *Good:* Star outlined, but point tips worn smooth; lettering, date, and numerals worn, but readable. *Fine:* Most details of design visible; lettering and date sharp. *Proof:* Coin should be in unused condition.

MINT MARK: On reverse, to right of Roman numerals.

Date	*Good*	*Fine*	*Amount Minted*
1851	$5.25	$ 7.00	5,447,400
1851-O	6.00	15.00	720,000
1852	5.25	7.00	18,663,500
1853	5.25	7.00	11,400,000
1854	6.50	7.00	671,000
1855	7.00	18.00	139,000
1856	6.50	7.00	1,458,000
1857	6.50	7.00	1,042,000
1858	6.50	7.00	1,604,000
1859	5.25	7.00	365,000
1860	5.25	7.00	287,000
1861	5.25	7.00	498,000
1862	5.25	7.00	363,550

	Proof	
1863	$1,100.00	460
1864	1,250.00	470
1865	1,250.00	500
1866	1,000.00	725
1867	1,000.00	625
1868	1,000.00	600
1869	1,000.00	600
1870	750.00	1,000

1871	750.00	960
1872	750.00	950
1873	1,100.00	600

NICKEL THREE-CENT PIECE

CONDITION: *V. Good:* Liberty outlined, but most details worn smooth; lettering and date worn but readable. *Fine:* Most details of design visible; all lettering and date sharp. *Proof:* Coin should be in unused condition.

MINT MARK: None.

Date	*V. Good*	*Fine*	*Amount Minted*
1865	$ 3.00	$ 3.50	11,382,000
1866	3.00	3.50	4,801,000
1867	3.00	3.50	3,915,000
1868	3.00	3.50	3,252,000
1869	3.00	3.50	1,604,000
1870	3.00	3.50	1,335,000
1871	3.00	3.50	604,000
1872	3.00	3.50	862,000
1873	3.00	3.50	1,173,000
1874	3.00	3.50	790,000
1875	4.00	6.00	228,000
1876	5.00	7.50	162,000
1879	20.00	27.50	25,300
1880	30.00	37.50	10,609
1881	3.50	4.00	1,080,575
1882	20.00	27.50	25,300
1883	30.00	37.50	10,609

1884	30.00	40.00	5,642
1885	30.00	40.00	4,790
1886	30.00	42.50	4,290
1887	42.50	62.50	7,961
1888	17.50	27.50	41,083
1889	17.50	27.50	21,561

	Proof	
1877	$1,250.00	510
1878	750.00	2,350
1887 with 87 over 86	650.00	2,960

10

FIVE-CENT PIECES

(Nickels)

Five-cent pieces were first struck in 1866. Like the nickel three-cent piece, this coin was issued originally to redeem fractional currency. However, the five-cent piece replaced the half dime and became one of our most widely used coins.

The first five-cent piece was the Shield type. It was composed of 75 parts copper to 25 parts nickel; this composition is still used today. The obverse of this coin closely resembles the large shield used on the obverse of the two-cent piece. The reverse shows a large 5 encircled by stars, rays, lettering, and the word CENTS beneath (the rays were later removed, resulting in a less crowded reverse).

In 1883, the Liberty Head nickel replaced the Shield type. The large 5 of the Shield nickel was replaced with the Roman numeral V, which was encircled with a wreath and lettering; the word CENTS was omitted. Because this coin was so similar in size and design to the half eagle (five-dollar gold piece), this five-cent piece was often illegally gold-plated and passed off as a five-dollar gold piece. During that same year, the lettering was rearranged and the word CENTS appeared on the coin.

Then in 1913, the Buffalo nickel was introduced. This handsome coin was designed by James E. Fraser. Two versions were struck in its first year of issue. The first type shows the buffalo standing on a hilly mound. The second type, which continued in later issues, shows the buffalo standing on a level plane. Buffalo nickels of the San Francisco and Denver Mints were often poorly struck, and with circulation, mint marks became almost indistinguishable. In 1937, this coin was so poorly struck at the Denver Mint that the buffalo appears to have only three legs. Because of this poor minting, coins showing readable S or D mint marks generally bring a higher premium than those coins struck at the Philadelphia Mint.

The Buffalo nickel was replaced with the Jefferson nickel in 1938. The Jefferson nickel is the only coin to show a mint mark for the Philadelphia Mint. This coin, designed by Felix Schlag, is still being issued.

SHIELD TYPE

with rays *without rays*

CONDITION: *Good:* Shield outlined, but most details worn; lettering and date worn but readable. *Fine:* Most details of design visible; all lettering and date sharp.

MINT MARK: None.

Date	*Good*	*Fine*	*Amount Minted*
1866	$ 4.50	$ 7.75	14,742,500
1867 with rays	5.00	8.75	30,909,500
1867 without rays	3.75	6.00	
1868	3.75	6.00	28,817,000

1869	3.75	6.00	16,395,000
1870	3.75	6.00	4,806,000
1871	19.00	35.00	561,000
1872	3.75	6.00	6,036,000
1873	3.75	6.00	4,550,000
1874	5.00	7.75	3,538,000
1875	9.00	16.50	2,097,000
1876	4.50	8.75	2,530,000
1879	30.00	45.00	29,100
1880	30.00	45.00	19,955
1881	22.50	37.50	72,375
1882	3.75	6.00	11,476,600
1883	3.75	6.00	1,456,919

	Proof	
1877	$1,600.00	510
1878	850.00	2,350

LIBERTY HEAD

without CENTS *with CENTS*

CONDITION: *Good:* Liberty outlined, but most details worn smooth; word LIBERTY on crown worn smooth; other lettering and date worn, but readable. *Fine:* Most details of design, word LIBERTY on crown visible; other lettering and date sharp.

MINT MARK: On reverse, to left of word CENTS.

Date	*Good*	*Fine*	*Amount Minted*
1883 without CENTS	$ 1.00	$ 1.25	5,479,519
1883	1.50	4.50	16,032,983
1884	3.00	5.25	11,273,942
1885	70.00	100.00	1,476,490
1886	22.50	45.00	3,330,290
1887	1.75	3.00	15,263,652
1888	3.25	5.50	10,720,483
1889	1.75	2.75	15,881,361
1890	1.75	3.50	16,259,272
1891	1.75	2.75	16,834,350
1892	1.75	3.25	11,699,642
1893	1.75	2.75	13,370,195
1894	3.00	5.50	5,413,132
1895	.80*	2.00	9,979,884
1896	.85*	4.50	8,842,920
1897	.20*	1.75	20,428,735
1898	.20*	1.75	12,532,087
1899	.20*	1.75	26,029,031
1900	.20*	.55*	27,255,995
1901	.20*	.55*	26,480,213
1902	.20*	.55*	31,480,579
1903	.20*	.55*	28,006,725
1904	.20*	.55*	21,404,984
1905	.20*	.55*	29,827,276
1906	.20*	.55*	38,613,725
1907	.20*	.55*	39,214,800
1908	.20*	.55*	22,686,177
1909	.20*	.55*	11,590,526
1910	.20*	.55*	30,169,353
1911	.20*	.55*	39,559,372
1912	.20*	.55*	26,236,714
1912-D	.50*	3.50	8,474,000
1912-S	15.00	22.50	238,000

** Coins marked with an asterisk are discussed on pages 25-26.*

BUFFALO NICKEL

buffalo on mound *buffalo on plane*

CONDITION: *Good:* Some details on buffalo and Indian head visible; horn on buffalo worn smooth; lettering and date readable. *Fine:* Most details, including buffalo horn, visible; all lettering and date sharp.

MINT MARK: On reverse, below the value.

Date	*Good*	*Fine*	*Amount Minted*
1913 buffalo on mound	$ .15*	$ .30*	30,993,520
1913 buffalo on plane	.20*	.50*	29,858,700
1913-D buffalo on mound	1.10	1.75	5,337,000
1913-D buffalo on plane	10.50	12.00	4,156,000
1913-S buffalo on mound	2.25	3.25	2,105,000
1913-S buffalo on plane	22.50	27.50	1,209,000
1914	.15*	.30*	20,665,738
1914-D	6.50	10.00	3,912,000
1914-S	1.75	3.75	3,470,000
1915	.45*	.75*	20,987,270
1915-D	1.75	4.50	7,569,500
1915-S	3.25	5.50	1,505,000
1916	.20*	.50*	63,498,066
1916-D	.60*	1.75	13,333,000
1916-S	1.10	1.75	11,860,000
1917	.20*	.45*	51,424,029
1917-D	1.50	3.25	9,910,800
1917-S	1.50	3.25	4,193,000
1918	.10*	.50*	32,086,314
1918-D	1.10	2.50	8,362,000
1918-D with 8 over 7	220.00	500.00	

* *Coins marked with an asterisk are discussed on pages 25-26.*

1918-S	1.50	2.50	4,882,000
1919	.10*	.40*	60,868,000
1919-D	1.50	3.00	8,006,000
1919-S	1.50	3.00	7,521,000
1920	.10*	.40*	63,093,000
1920-D	1.00	2.00	9,418,000
1920-S	1.00	2.00	9,689,000
1921	.10*	.65*	10,663,000
1921-S	5.00	10.00	1,557,000
1923	.10*	.40*	35,715,000
1923-S	1.00	3.00	6,142,000
1924	.10*	.40*	21,620,000
1924-D	1.00	2.00	5,258,000
1924-S	1.25	4.00	1,437,000
1925	.10*	.40*	35,565,100
1925-D	1.00	3.50	4,450,000
1925-S	1.00	3.50	6,256,000
1926	.10*	.15*	44,693,000
1926-D	1.00	1.10	5,638,000
1926-S	2.00	5.00	970,000
1927	.10*	.15*	37,981,000
1927-D	.45*	.95*	5,730,000
1927-S	.90*	1.75	3,430,000
1928	.10*	.15*	23,411,000
1928-D	.10*	.35*	6,436,000
1928-S	.10*	.40*	6,936,000
1929	.10*	.15*	36,446,000
1929-D	.10*	.35*	8,370,000
1929-S	.10*	.15*	7,754,000
1930	.10*	.15*	22,849,000
1930-S	.10*	.45*	5,435,000
1931-S	2.00	3.00	1,200,000
1934	.10*	.15*	20,213,003
1934-D	.10*	.30*	7,480,000
1935	.10*	.15*	58,264,000
1935-D	.10*	.15*	12,092,000
1935-S	.10*	.15*	10,300,000
1936	.10*	.15*	119,001,420
1936-D	.10*	.15*	24,418,000

** Coins marked with an asterisk are discussed on pages 25-26.*

1936-S	.10*	.15*	14,930,000
1937	.10*	.15*	79,485,769
1937-D	.10*	.15*	17,826,000
1937-D with three-legged buffalo	50.00	90.00	
1937-S	.10*	.25*	5,635,000
1938-D	.10*	.15*	7,020,000

JEFFERSON NICKEL

CONDITION: *V. Good:* Most details of Jefferson head and building visible; all lettering and date sharp. *V. Fine:* Signs of wear on cheekbone, other details sharp; lettering and date sharp.

MINT MARK: 1938-64: On reverse, to right of building or above dome; 1968—: On obverse.

Date	*V. Good*	*V. Fine*	*Minted*
1938	$ .05	$ .05	19,515,365
1938-D	.45*	.65*	5,376,000
1938-S	.80*	1.00	4,105,000
1939	.05	.05	120,627,535
1939-D	1.25	1.75	3,514,000
1939-S	.40*	.80*	6,630,000
1940	.05	.05	176,499,158
1940-D	.05	.05	43,540,000
1940-S	.05	.05	39,690,000
1941	.05	.05	203,283,720
1941-D	.05	.05	53,432,000

* *Coins marked with an asterisk are discussed on pages 25-26.*

1941-S	.05	.05	43,445,000
1942	.05	.05	49,818,600
1942-D	.25*	.35*	13,938,000
1942-P	.30*	.40*	57,900,600
1942-S	.30*	.40*	32,900,000
1943-P	.30*	.40*	271,165,000
1943-D	.30*	.40*	15,294,000
1943-S	.30*	.40*	104,060,000
1944-P	.30*	.40*	119,150,000
1944-D	.30*	.40*	32,309,000
1944-S	.30*	.40*	21,640,000
1945-P	.30*	.40*	119,408,100
1945-D	.30*	.40*	37,158,000
1945-S	.30*	.40*	58,939,000
1946	.05	.05	161,116,000
1946-D	.05	.05	45,292,200
1946-S	.05	.05	13,560,000
1947	.05	.05	95,000,000
1947-D	.05	.05	37,882,000
1947-S	.05	.05	24,720,000
1948	.05	.05	89,348,000
1948-D	.05	.05	44,734,000
1948-S	.05	.05	11,300,000
1949	.05	.05	60,652,000
1949-D	.05	.05	35,238,000
1949-S	.05	.05	9,716,000
1950	.05	.05	9,847,386
1950-D	2.00	3.50	2,630,030
1951	.05	.05	28,689,500
1951-D	.05	.05	20,460,000
1951-S	.05	.25*	7,776,000
1952	.05	.05	64,069,980
1952-D	.05	.05	30,638,000
1952-S	.05	.05	20,572,000
1953	.05	.05	46,772,800
1953-D	.05	.05	59,878,600
1953-S	.05	.05	19,210,900
1954	.05	.05	47,917,350
1954-D	.05	.05	117,183,060

** Coins marked with an asterisk are discussed on pages 25-26.*

1954-S	.05	.05	29,384,000
1955	.15*	.25*	8,266,200
1955-D	.05	.05	74,464,100
1956	.05	.05	35,885,384
1956-D	.05	.05	67,222,940
1957	.05	.05	39,655,952
1957-D	.05	.05	136,828,900
1958	.05	.05	17,963,652
1958-D	.05	.05	168,249,120
1959	.05	.05	28,397,291
1959-D	.05	.05	160,738,240
1960	.05	.05	57,107,602
1960-D	.05	.05	192,582,180
1961	.05	.05	76,668,244
1961-D	.05	.05	229,342,760
1962	.05	.05	100,602,019
1962-D	.05	.05	280,195,720
1963	.05	.05	175,776,000
1963-D	.05	.05	276,829,460
1964	.05	.05	1,028,622,762
1964-D	.05	.05	1,787,297,160
1965	.05	.05	136,131,380
1966	.05	.05	156,208,283
1967	.05	.05	107,325,800
1968-D	.05	.05	91,227,880
1968-S	.05	.05	103,437,510
1969-D	.05	.05	202,807,500
1969-S	.05	.05	123,099,631
1970-D	.05	.05	515,485,380
1970-S	.05	.05	241,464,814
1971	.05	.05	106,884,000
1971-D	.05	.05	316,144,800
1972	.05	.05	202,036,000
1972-D	.05	.05	351,694,600
1973-1982	.05	.05	———

* *Coins marked with an asterisk are discussed on pages 25-26.*

11

HALF DIMES

Half dimes were struck in silver from 1794 to 1873. The value did not appear on the coin until 1829 when "5 C." was added to the reverse. In 1837, with the Liberty Seated type, the words HALF DIME were added to designate the value.

This was a widely used coin and is still popular among collectors. Even so, the half dime was replaced with an even more popular coin of the same denomination, the five-cent piece (see page 59).

Four basic types of half dimes were issued: Liberty with Flowing Hair (1794–95); Liberty with Draped Bust (1796–1805); Liberty with Turban (1829–37); Liberty Seated (1837–73).

LIBERTY WITH FLOWING HAIR

CONDITION: *Good:* Liberty outlined but most details worn;

most lettering and date readable. *Fine:* Some details of design visible; all lettering and date sharp.

MINT MARK: None.

Date	*Good*	*Fine*	*Amount Minted*
1794	$340.00	$825.00	84,416
1795	300.00	600.00	

LIBERTY WITH DRAPED BUST

with small eagle

CONDITION: *Good:* Liberty outlined, but most details worn smooth; most lettering and date readable. *Fine:* Most details of hair and drapery visible; lettering and date sharp.

MINT MARK: None.

Date	*Good*	*Fine*	*Amount Minted*
1796	$375.00	$750.00	10,230
1797 with 15 stars	375.00	750.00	44,527
1797 with 16 stars	375.00	750.00	
1797 with 13 stars	375.00	750.00	

with LIBEKTY

with large eagle

Date	*Good*	*Fine*	*Amount Minted*
1800	$ 285.00	$ 500.00	24,000
1800 with LIBEKTY	285.00	500.00	
1801	285.00	500.00	33,910
1802	2,500.00	5,250.00	13,910
1803	285.00	390.00	37,850
1805	330.00	700.00	15,600

LIBERTY WITH TURBAN

CONDITION: *Good:* Liberty outlined but most details worn smooth; most lettering and date readable. *Fine:* Most details of design visible; word LIBERTY on headband readable; other lettering and date sharp.

MINT MARK: None.

Date	*Good*	*Fine*	*Amount Minted*
1829	$8.50	$18.00	1,230,000
1830	8.50	18.00	1,240,000
1831	8.50	18.00	1,242,700
1832	8.50	18.00	965,000
1833	8.50	18.00	1,370,000
1834	8.50	18.00	1,480,000
1835	8.50	18.00	2,760,000
1836	8.50	18.00	1,900,000
1837	8.50	18.00	2,276,000

LIBERTY SEATED

without stars

CONDITION: *Good:* Liberty and wreath outlined with some details visible; most lettering and date readable. *Fine:* Most details and word LIBERTY on shield visible; other lettering and date sharp.

MINT MARK: On reverse, below the value (below or within wreath).

Date	*Good*	*Fine*	*Amount Minted*
1837	$15.00	$25.00	2,255,000
1838-O	35.00	90.00	———

with stars *with arrows at date*

Date	*Good*	*Fine*	*Amount Minted*
1838	$ 3.25	$ 4.00	2,555,000
1839	3.25	4.00	1,069,150
1839-O	3.25	5.00	1,096,550
1840	3.25	4.00	1,344,085
1840-O	3.25	8.50	935,000
1841	3.25	4.00	1,150,000
1841-O	3.25	4.00	815,000
1842	3.25	4.00	815,000

1842-O	8.00	20.00	350,000
1843	3.25	5.00	1,165,000
1844	3.25	5.00	430,000
1844-O	12.00	30.00	220,000
1845	3.25	5.00	1,564,000
1846	40.00	100.00	27,000
1847	3.25	5.00	1,274,000
1848	3.25	5.00	668,000
1848-O	3.25	7.00	600,000
1849	3.25	5.00	1,309,000
1849-O	20.00	45.00	140,000
1850	3.25	5.00	955,000
1850-O	3.25	5.00	690,000
1851	3.25	5.00	781,000
1851-O	3.25	5.00	860,000
1852	3.25	5.00	1,000,500
1852-O	3.25	8.50	260,000
1853 with arrows	3.25	5.00	13,345,020
1853 without arrows	5.00	12.00	
1853-O with arrows	3.25	5.00	2,360,000
1853-O without arrows	85.00	130.00	
1854 with arrows	3.25	5.00	5,740,000
1854-O with arrows	3.25	5.00	1,560,000
1855 with arrows	3.25	5.00	1,750,000
1855-O with arrows	5.00	8.00	600,000
1856	3.25	5.00	4,880,000
1856-O	3.25	5.00	1,100,000
1857	3.25	5.00	7,280,000
1857-O	3.25	5.00	1,380,000
1858	3.25	5.00	3,500,000
1858-O	3.25	5.00	1,600,000
1859	3.25	5.00	340,000
1859-O	3.25	5.00	560,000

	Proof	
1859 with reverse of 1860 (see below)	$6,000.00	———
1860 with obverse of 1859 (see below)	2,000.00	100

with legend

Date	Good	Fine	Amount Minted
1860	$ 3.25	$ 5.00	799,000
1860-O	3.25	5.00	1,060,000
1861	3.25	5.00	3,281,000
1862	3.25	5.00	1,492,550
1863	25.00	32.50	18,460
1863-S	6.00	10.00	100,000
1864	40.00	65.00	——
1864-S	8.00	12.50	90,000
1865	25.00	40.00	13,500
1865-S	5.00	12.00	120,000
1866	25.00	40.00	10,725
1866-S	4.00	6.50	120,000
1867	32.50	40.00	8,625
1867-S	4.00	6.50	120,000
1868	5.00	9.00	85,900
1868-S	3.25	5.00	280,000
1869	3.25	5.00	208,600
1869-S	3.25	5.00	230,000
1870	3.25	5.00	536,600
1871	3.25	5.00	1,488,860
1871-S	5.00	10.00	161,000
1872	3.25	5.00	2,947,950
1872-S with S below wreath	3.25	5.00	837,000
1872-S with S within wreath	3.25	5.00	
1873	3.25	5.00	712,600
1873-S	3.25	5.00	324,000

12

DIMES

Dimes were first struck in silver in 1796. Early dimes did not show a face value until 1809, when "10 C." was added to the reverse; in 1837, the value ONE DIME was spelled out in full.

Before 1892, designs of this denomination closely followed those of the half dime. Early types of dimes include Liberty with Draped Bust (1796–1807); Liberty with Turban (1809–37); Liberty Seated (1837–91).

The Liberty Head dime, introduced in 1892, is also known as the "Barber" dime, after its designer, Charles E. Barber. The designer used this same obverse on the quarter dollar and half dollar issued the same year.

The Mercury dime replaced the Liberty Head dime in 1916. This coin, designed by A. A. Weinman, shows a strong Roman influence. On the obverse is a Liberty with wings, symbolic of free thought. A fasces, symbolic of consular authority, is on the reverse.

The Roosevelt dime was issued in 1946 to honor the late president. This coin, designed by John R. Sinnock, is still being issued.

Note: *Prices for "common" silver dimes are based on the price of silver. For details, see page 26.*

LIBERTY WITH DRAPED BUST

with small eagle *with large eagle*

CONDITION: *Good:* Liberty outlined but most details worn smooth; most lettering and date readable. *Fine:* Most hair and drapery details visible; all lettering and date sharp.

MINT MARK: None.

Date	*Good*	*Fine*	*Amount Minted*
1796 small eagle	$650.00	$1,150.00	22,135
1797 with 16 stars	575.00	1,075.00	25,261
1797 with 13 stars	575.00	1,075.00	
1798 large eagle	225.00	350.00	27,550
1798 with 8 over 7	225.00	350.00	
1800	200.00	300.00	21,760
1801	200.00	325.00	34,640
1802	200.00	350.00	10,975
1803	200.00	300.00	33,040
1804	235.00	450.00	8,265
1805	180.00	275.00	120,780
1807	180.00	275.00	165,000

LIBERTY WITH TURBAN

CONDITION: *Good:* Liberty outlined but most details worn smooth; word LIBERTY on headband partly visible; other lettering and date readable. *Fine:* Most details and word LIBERTY visible, other lettering and date sharp.

MINT MARK: None.

Date	Good	Fine	Amount Minted
1809	$35.00	$60.00	44,710
1811 with 11 over 09	20.00	50.00	65,180
1814	12.50	20.00	421,500
1820	12.50	20.00	942,587
1821	12.50	20.00	1,186,512
1822	30.00	60.00	100,000
1823	12.50	20.00	440,000
1824 with 4 over 2	12.50	25.00	———
1825	12.50	20.00	510,000
1827	12.50	20.00	1,215,000
1828 with large date	12.50	30.00	125,000
1828 with small date	10.00	20.00	
1829	10.00	16.50	770,000
1829 with large 10 C	10.00	22.50	
1830	10.00	16.50	510,000
1831	10.00	16.50	771,350
1832	10.00	16.50	522,500
1833	10.00	16.50	285,000
1834	10.00	16.50	635,000
1835	10.00	16.50	1,410,000
1836	10.00	16.50	1,190,000
1837	10.00	16.50	1,042,000

LIBERTY SEATED

without stars *with stars*

CONDITION: *Good:* Liberty outlined but most details worn; most lettering readable. *Fine:* Most details of design and word LIBERTY visible; other lettering and date sharp.

MINT MARK: Reverse, below or within wreath.

Date	*Good*	*Fine*	*Amount Minted*
1837 without stars	$16.50	$35.00	included above
1838	4.00	5.00	1,992,500
1838-O without stars	20.00	52.50	402,434
1839	4.00	5.00	1,053,115
1839-O	4.00	5.00	1,243,272
1840	4.00	5.00	1,358,580
1840-O	4.00	5.00	1,175,000
1841	4.00	5.00	1,622,500
1841-O	4.00	5.00	2,007,500
1842	4.00	5.00	1,887,500
1842-O	4.00	5.00	2,020,000
1843	4.00	5.00	1,370,000
1843-O	12.50	32.50	150,000
1844	20.00	45.00	72,500
1845	4.00	5.00	1,755,000
1845-O	8.00	15.50	230,000
1846	25.00	45.00	31,300
1847	4.00	5.00	245,000
1848	4.00	5.00	451,500
1849	4.00	5.00	839,000
1849-O	6.50	12.50	300,000
1850	4.00	5.00	1,931,500
1850-O	4.00	6.50	510,000
1851	4.00	5.00	1,026,500
1851-O	4.00	6.50	400,000
1852	4.00	5.00	1,535,500
1852-O	4.00	8.00	430,000
1853	12.50	25.00	12,173,010
1853 with arrows at date	4.00	5.00	
1853-O with arrows	4.00	5.00	1,100,000
1854 with arrows	4.00	5.00	4,470,000
1854-O with arrows	4.00	5.00	1,770,000
1855 with arrows	4.00	5.00	2,075,000
1856	4.00	5.00	5,780,000
1856-O	4.00	5.00	1,180,000
1856-S	25.00	45.00	70,000

1857	4.00	5.00	5,580,000
1857-O	4.00	5.00	1,540,000
1858	4.00	5.00	1,540,000
1858-O	4.00	5.00	290,000
1858-S	20.00	40.00	60,000
1859	4.00	5.00	430,000
1859-O	4.00	5.00	480,000
1859-S	20.00	40.00	60,000
1860-S	12.50	20.00	140,000

	Proof	
1859 reverse of 1860 (see below)	$4,000.00	———

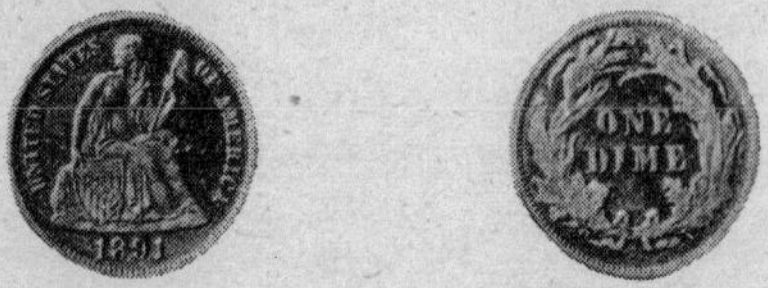

with legend

Date	*Good*	*Fine*	*Amount Minted*
1860	$ 4.25	$ 6.00	607,000
1860-O	110.00	180.00	40,000
1861	3.50	5.00	1,924,000
1861-S	9.50	27.50	172,500
1862	3.50	5.00	847,550
1862-S	11.00	30.00	180,750
1863	50.00	65.00	14,460
1863-S	9.50	20.00	157,500
1864	45.00	60.00	39,070
1864-S	12.50	20.00	230,000
1865	55.00	75.00	10,500
1865-S	12.50	30.00	175,000
1866	55.00	75.00	8,725
1866-S	9.50	20.00	135,000
1867	65.00	80.00	6,625
1867-S	9.50	20.00	140,000
1868	4.25	7.50	466,250
1868-S	5.75	15.00	260,000

1869	5.50	7.50	256,600
1869-S	3.50	7.50	450,000
1870	4.00	5.50	471,500
1870-S	30.00	62.50	50,000
1871	3.50	5.00	753,610
1871-CC	110.00	300.00	20,100
1871-S	7.50	15.00	320,000
1872	3.50	5.00	2,396,450
1872-CC	90.00	225.00	24,000
1872-S	6.00	13.50	190,000
1873	3.50	5.00	1,568,600
1873 with arrows at date	5.50	11.50	2,378,500
1873-CC with arrows	225.00	500.00	18,791
1873-S with arrows	7.50	15.00	455,000
1874 with arrows	5.50	11.50	2,940,700
1874-CC with arrows	150.00	300.00	10,817
1874-S with arrows	7.50	15.00	240,000
1875	3.50	5.00	10,350,700
1875-CC	3.50	5.00	4,645,000
1875-S	3.50	5.00	9,070,000
1876	3.50	5.00	11,461,150
1876-CC	3.50	5.00	8,270,000
1876-S	3.50	5.00	10,420,000
1877	3.50	5.00	7,310,510
1877-CC	3.50	5.00	7,700,000
1877-S	3.50	5.00	2,340,000
1878	3.50	5.00	1,678,800
1878-CC	6.00	15.00	200.000
1879	30.00	50.00	15,100
1880	25.00	45.00	37,355
1881	30.00	50.00	24,975
1882	3.50	5.00	3,911,100
1883	3.50	5.00	7,675,712
1884	3.50	5.00	3,366,380
1884-S	3.50	7.50	564,969
1885	3.50	5.00	2,533,427
1885-S	30.00	47.50	43,690
1886	3.50	5.00	6,377,570
1886-S	3.50	6.50	206,524
1887	3.50	5.00	11,283,939
1887-S	3.50	5.00	4,454,450

1888	3.50	5.00	5,496,487
1888-S	3.50	5.00	1,720,000
1889	3.50	5.00	7,380,711
1889-S	5.00	9.00	972,678
1890	3.50	5.00	9,911,541
1890-S	3.50	5.00	1,423,076
1891	3.50	5.00	15,310,600
1891-O	3.50	5.00	4,540,000
1891-S	3.50	5.00	3,196,116

LIBERTY HEAD

CONDITION: *Good:* Liberty outlined but most details worn; most lettering readable. *Fine:* Most details of design and word LIBERTY visible; other lettering and date sharp.

MINT MARK: On reverse, below the wreath.

Date	*Good*	*Fine*	*Amount Minted*
1892	$ 1.25*	$ 1.50*	12,121,245
1892-O	1.00	1.75	3,841,700
1892-S	5.00	10.00	990,710
1893	1.25*	1.75*	3,340,792
1893-O	1.50	4.00	1,760,000
1893-S	1.50	4.00	2,491,401
1894	1.50*	1.75	1,330,972
1894-O	9.00	25.00	720,000
1895	7.50	15.00	690,880
1895-O	17.50	45.00	440,000
1895-S	2.75	8.50	1,120,000
1896	1.50*	1.50*	2,000,762
1896-O	8.00	15.00	610,000
1896-S	10.00	19.00	575,056

** Coins marked with an asterisk are discussed on pages 25-26.*

1897	1.25*	1.50*	10,869,264
1897-O	9.00	17.00	666,000
1897-S	2.25	7.00	1,342,844
1898	1.25*	1.50*	16,320,735
1898-O	2.00*	3.25	2,130,000
1898-S	2.00*	2.75	1,702,507
1899	1.25*	1.50*	19,580,846
1899-O	2.00*	4.00	2,650,000
1899-S	2.00*	4.00	1,867,493
1900	1.25*	1.50*	17,600,912
1900-O	2.00*	4.00	2,010,000
1900-S	1.50*	2.50	5,168,270
1901	1.25*	1.50*	18,860,478
1901-O	1.25*	2.75	5,620,000
1901-S	7.50	30.00	593,022
1902	1.25*	1.50*	21,380,777
1902-O	1.25*	2.25	4,500,000
1902-S	2.00*	4.00	2,070,000
1903	1.25*	1.50*	19,500,755
1903-O	1.25*	1.75*	8,180,000
1903-S	3.25	7.00	613,300
1904	1.25*	1.50*	14,601,207
1904-S	2.75	7.00	800,000
1905	1.25*	1.50*	14,552,350
1905-O	1.25*	1.75*	3,400,000
1905-S	1.25*	1.75*	6,855,199
1906	1.25*	1.50*	19,958,406
1906-D	1.25*	1.50*	4,060,000
1906-O	1.25*	2.00*	2,610,000
1906-S	1.25*	2.00*	3,136,640
1907	1.25*	1.50*	22,220,575
1907-D	1.25*	2.00*	4,080,000
1907-O	1.25*	1.50*	5,058,000
1907-S	1.25*	1.50*	3,178,470
1908	1.25*	1.50*	10,600,545
1908-D	1.25*	1.50*	7,490,000
1908-O	1.25*	2.00*	1,789,000
1908-S	1.25*	2.00*	3,220,000
1909	1.25*	1.50*	10,240,650
1909-D	1.75*	3.00	954,000

* *Coins marked with an asterisk are discussed on pages 25-26.*

1909-O	1.75*	3.25	2,287,000
1909-S	1.75*	3.25	1,000,000
1910	1.25*	1.50*	11,520,551
1910-D	1.25*	1.50*	3,490,000
1910-S	1.25*	1.50*	1,240,000
1911	1.25*	1.50*	18,870,543
1911-D	1.25*	1.50*	11,209,000
1911-S	1.25*	2.00*	3,520,000
1912	1.25*	1.50*	19,350,700
1912-D	1.25*	1.50*	11,760,000
1912-S	1.25*	2.00*	3,420,000
1913	1.25*	1.50*	19,760,622
1913-S	2.00	8.00	510,000
1914	1.25*	1.50*	17,360,655
1914-D	1.25*	1.50*	11,908,000
1914-S	1.25*	2.00*	2,100,000
1915	1.25*	1.50*	5,620,450
1915-S	1.50*	2.00*	960,000
1916	1.25*	1.50*	18,490,000
1916-S	1.25*	1.50*	5,820,000

** Coins marked with an asterisk are discussed on pages 25-26.*

MERCURY DIME

CONDITION: *Good:* Mercury and fasces outlined but most details worn; lettering and date readable. *Fine:* Most details of design visible; all lettering and date sharp.

MINT MARK: On reverse, lower left of fasces.

Date	*Good*	*Fine*	*Amount Minted*
1916	$ 1.25*	$ 1.50*	22,180,080
1916-D	110.00	200.00	264,000
1916-S	1.25*	1.75*	10,450,000
1917	1.25*	1.50*	55,230,000

1917-D	1.25*	1.50*	9,402,000
1917-S	1.25*	1.50*	27,330,000
1918	1.25*	1.50*	26,680,000
1918-D	1.25*	1.50*	22,674,800
1918-S	1.25*	1.50*	19,300,000
1919	1.25*	1.50*	35,740,000
1919-D	1.50*	1.75	9,939,000
1919-S	1.50*	1.75	8,850,000
1920	1.25*	1.50*	59,030,000
1920-D	1.25*	1.50*	19,171,000
1920-S	1.25*	1.50*	13,820,000
1921	7.50	25.00	1,230,000
1921-D	12.50	35.00	1,080,000
1923	1.25*	1.50*	50,130,000
1923-S	1.25*	2.00*	6,440,000
1924	1.25*	1.50*	24,010,000
1924-D	1.25*	1.50*	6,810,000
1924-S	1.25*	1.50*	7,120,000
1925	1.25*	1.50*	25,610,000
1925-D	1.50*	1.75*	5,117,000
1925-S	1.25*	1.50*	5,850,000
1926	1.25*	1.50*	32,160,000
1926-D	1.25*	1.50*	6,828,000
1926-S	1.75	3.50	1,520,000
1927	1.25*	1.50*	28,080,000
1927-D	1.25*	1.50*	4,812,000
1927-S	1.25*	1.50*	4,770,000
1928	1.25*	1.50*	19,480,000
1928-D	1.25*	1.50*	4,161,000
1928-S	1.25*	1.50*	7,400,000
1929	1.25*	1.50*	25,970,000
1929-D	1.25*	1.50*	5,034,000
1929-S	1.25*	1.50*	4,730,000
1930	1.25*	1.50*	6,770,000
1930-S	1.50	1.75	1,843,000
1931	1.25*	1.50*	3,150,000
1931-D	2.00	2.50	1,260,000
1931-S	1.50	2.00	1,800,000
1934	1.25*	1.50*	24,080,000

** Coins marked with an asterisk are discussed on pages 25-26.*

1934-D	1.25*	1.50*	6,772,000
1935	1.25*	1.50*	58,830,000
1935-D	1.25*	1.50*	10,477,000
1935-S	1.25*	1.50*	15,840,000
1936	1.25*	1.50*	87,504,130
1936-D	1.25*	1.50*	16,132,000
1936-S	1.25*	1.50*	9,210,000
1937	1.25*	1.50*	56,865,756
1937-D	1.25*	1.50*	14,146,000
1937-S	1.25*	1.50*	9,740,000
1938	1.25*	1.50*	22,198,728
1938-D	1.25*	1.50*	5,537,000
1938-S	1.25*	1.50*	8,090,000
1939	1.25*	1.50*	67,749,321
1939-D	1.25*	1.50*	24,394,000
1939-S	1.25*	1.50*	10,540,000
1940	1.25*	1.50*	65,361,827
1940-D	1.25*	1.50*	21,198,000
1940-S	1.25*	1.50*	21,560,000
1941	1.25*	1.50*	175,106,557
1941-D	1.25*	1.50*	45,634,000
1941-S	1.25*	1.50*	43,090,000
1942	1.25*	1.50*	205,432,329
1942 with 2 over 1 (see photograph on page 22)	75.00	100.00	
1942-D	1.25*	1.50*	60,740,000
1942-S	1.25*	1.50*	49,300,000
1943	1.25*	1.50*	191,710,000
1943-D	1.25*	1.50*	71,949,000
1943-S	1.25*	1.50*	60,400,000
1944	1.25*	1.50*	231,410,000
1944-D	1.25*	1.50*	62,224,000
1944-S	1.25*	1.50*	49,490,000
1945	1.25*	1.50*	159,130,000
1945-D	1.25*	1.50*	40,245,000
1945-S	1.25*	1.50*	41,920,000

* *Coins marked with an asterisk are discussed on pages 25-26.*

ROOSEVELT DIME

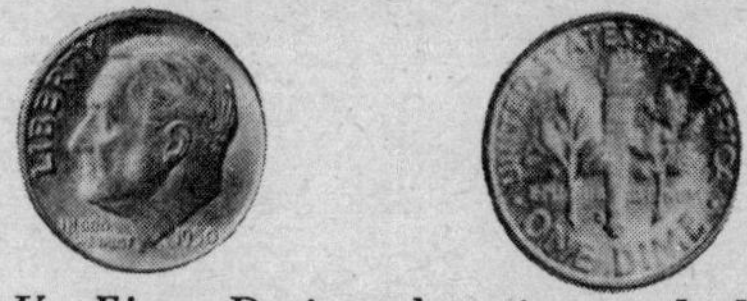

CONDITION: *V. Fine:* Design, lettering and date sharp.
MINT MARK: 1946–64: On reverse; 1968—: On obverse.

Date	*V. Fine*	*Amount Minted*
1946	$1.25*	255,250,000
1946-D	1.25*	61,043,500
1946-S	1.25*	27,990,000
1947	1.25*	121,520,000
1947-D	1.25*	46,835,000
1947-S	1.25*	34,840,000
1948	1.25*	74,950,000
1948-D	1.25*	52,841,000
1948-S	1.25*	35,520,000
1949	1.25*	30,940,000
1949-D	1.25*	26,034,000
1949-S	1.25*	13,510,000
1950	1.25*	50,181,500
1950-D	1.25*	46,803,000
1950-S	1.25*	20,440,000
1951	1.25*	103,937,602
1951-D	1.25*	52,191,800
1951-S	1.25*	31,630,000
1952	1.25*	99,122,073
1952-D	1.25*	122,100,000
1952-S	1.25*	44,419,500
1953	1.25*	53,618,920
1953-D	1.25*	136,433,000
1953-S	1.25*	39,180,000
1954	1.25*	114,243,503
1954-D	1.25*	106,397,000
1954-S	1.25*	22,860,000
1955	1.25*	12,828,381

* *Coins marked with an asterisk are discussed on pages 25-26.*

1955-D	1.25*	13,959,000
1955-S	1.25*	18,510,000
1956	1.25*	109,309,384
1956-D	1.25*	108,015,100
1957	1.25*	161,407,952
1957-D	1.25*	113,354,330
1958	1.25*	32,785,652
1958-D	1.25*	136,564,600
1959	1.25*	86,929,291
1959-D	1.25*	164,919,790
1960	1.25*	72,081,602
1960-D	1.25*	200,160,400
1961	1.25*	93,730,000
1961-D	1.25*	209,146,550
1962	1.25*	75,668,019
1962-D	1.25*	334,948,380
1963	1.25*	123,650,000
1963-D	1.25*	421,476,530
1964	1.25*	933,310,762
1964-D	1.25*	1,189,611,550
1965	.10	1,922,936,200
1966	.10	1,382,734,540
1967	.10	2,244,007,320
1968	.10	424,470,400
1968-D	.10	480,748,280
1969	.10	145,790,000
1969-D	.10	563,323,870
1970	.10	345,570,000
1970-D	.10	754,942,100
1971	.10	162,690,000
1971-D	.10	377,914,240
1972	.10	431,540,000
1972-D	.10	330,290,000
1973-1982	.10	———

** Coins marked with an asterisk are discussed on pages 25-26.*

13

TWENTY-CENT PIECES

The twenty-cent piece was struck in silver from 1875 to 1878. It was one of the most unpopular and shortest-lived coins ever issued by the U. S. Mint for general circulation. The reason for its extreme unpopularity was its similarity, both in size and in design, to the quarter dollar of the same years. During its last two years of issue, the twenty-cent piece was struck in proof only.

The Liberty Seated type was the only twenty-cent piece issued. This coin was struck with a smooth edge.

CONDITION: *Good:* Liberty and eagle outlined, but most details worn smooth; lettering and date readable. *Fine:* Most details of design and word LIBERTY on shield visible; other lettering and date sharp. *Proof:* Coin should be in unused condition.

MINT MARK: On reverse, below the eagle.

Date	*Good*	*Fine*	*Amount Minted*
1875	$ 30.00	$ 40.00	39,700
1875-CC	30.00	40.00	133,290
1875-S	27.50	35.00	1,155,000
1876	32.50	42.50	15,900
1876-CC	5,000.00	10,000.00	10,000

	Proof	
1877	$2,500.00	510
1878	2,000.00	600

14

QUARTER DOLLARS

Quarter dollars were first struck in silver in 1796. Early quarters showed no value until 1804, when "25 C." appeared on the reverse. In 1838, the words QUAR. DOL. were added to designate the value.

Early types of quarter dollars are: Liberty with Draped Bust (1796–1807); Liberty with Turban (1815–38); and Liberty Seated (1838–91). In 1831, the diameter of the quarter dollar was reduced to its present size.

In 1892, the Liberty Head quarter was introduced. This coin is also called the "Barber" quarter after its designer, Charles E. Barber. With this coin, the value QUARTER DOLLAR was spelled out in full.

The Liberty Standing quarter replaced the Liberty Head quarter in 1916. This coin was designed by Herman A. MacNeil. Prior to 1925, the date was struck too high in relief, causing rapid wear with circulation. In 1925, the date was lowered and the problem was eliminated. Dates before 1925 are difficult to distinguish unless the coin is in very good condition.

In 1932, on the bicentennial of George Washington's birthday, the Washington quarter dollar was introduced. This coin, designed by John Flanagan, is still being issued.

Note: *Prices for "common" silver quarters are based on the price of silver.* *For details, see page 26.*

LIBERTY WITH DRAPED BUST

with small eagle

CONDITION: *Good:* Liberty and eagle outlined but most details worn smooth; lettering and date readable. *Fine:* Most details of design visible; lettering and date sharp.

MINT MARK: None.

Date	*Good*	*Fine*	*Amount Minted*
1796	$1,750.00	$3,500.00	5,894

with large eagle

Date	*Good*	*Fine*	*Amount Minted*
1804	$150.00	$300.00	6,738
1805	82.50	250.00	121,394
1806	82.50	250.00	206,124
1807	82.50	250.00	220,643

LIBERTY WITH TURBAN

CONDITION: *Good:* Liberty outlined with some details visible; lettering and date readable. *Fine:* Most details of design and word LIBERTY on headband visible; other lettering and date sharp.

MINT MARK: None.

Date	*Good*	*Fine*	*Amount Minted*
1815	$ 27.50	$ 60.00	69,232
1818	27.50	60.00	361,174
1819	27.50	60.00	144,000
1820	27.50	60.00	127,444
1821	27.50	60.00	216,851
1822	27.50	60.00	} 64,080
1822 with 25 over 50 on reverse	120.00	270.00	}
1823 with 3 over 2	1,500.00	3,500.00	17,800
1824	27.50	60.00	———
1825	27.50	60.00	168,000
1828	27.50	60.00	102,000

	Proof	
1827 Original, curled base 2 in 25¢	$25,000.00	} 4,000
1827 Restrike, square base 2 in 25¢	6,000.00	}

reduced size

Date	*Good*	*Fine*	*Amount Minted*
1831	$27.50	$42.50	398,000
1832	27.50	42.50	320,000
1833	27.50	42.50	156,000
1834	27.50	42.50	286,000
1835	27.50	42.50	1,952,000
1836	27.50	42.50	472,000
1837	27.50	42.50	252,400
1838	27.50	42.50	832,000

LIBERTY SEATED

with arrows at date

with rays behind eagle

CONDITION: *Good:* Liberty outlined with most details visible; most lettering and date readable. *Fine:* Most details of design and word LIBERTY on shield visible; other lettering and date sharp.

MINT MARK: On reverse, below the eagle.

Date	*Good*	*Fine*	*Amount Minted*
1838	$ 7.50	$12.00	included above
1839	7.50	10.00	491,146
1840	7.50	10.00	188,127
1840-O	7.50	10.00	425,200
1840-O with drapery at elbow	7.50	10.00	
1841	9.00	18.00	120,000
1841-O	7.50	10.00	452,000
1842	15.00	25.00	88,000
1842-O	7.50	10.00	769,000
1843	7.50	10.00	645,600
1843-O	7.50	10.00	968,000
1844	7.50	10.00	421,200
1844-O	7.50	10.00	740,000
1845	7.50	10.00	922,000
1846	7.50	10.00	510,000
1847	7.50	10.00	734,000
1847-O	7.50	10.00	368,000
1848	15.00	27.50	146,000
1849	7.50	10.00	340,000
1849-O	70.00	150.00	——
1850	7.50	10.00	190,800
1850-O	7.50	10.00	412,000
1851	9.00	17.50	160,000
1851-O	9.00	17.50	88,000
1852	9.00	15.00	177,060
1852-O	25.00	50.00	96,000
1853 with 3 over 2	35.00	65.00	15,254,220
1853 with arrows and rays	7.50	10.00	

1853-O with arrows and rays	7.50	10.00	1,332,000
1854	7.50	8.50	12,380,000
1854-O	7.50	8.50	1,484,000
1855	7.50	8.50	2,857,000
1855-O	35.00	65.00	176,000
1855-S	30.00	65.00	396,400
1856	7.50	8.50	7,264,000
1856-O	7.50	8.50	968,000
1856-S	14.00	27.50	286,000
1857	7.50	8.50	9,644,000
1857-O	7.50	8.50	1,180,000
1857-S	14.00	27.50	82,000
1858	7.50	8.50	7,368,000
1858-O	7.50	8.50	520,000
1858-S	15.00	27.50	121,000
1859	7.50	8.50	1,344,000
1859-O	7.50	8.50	260,000
1859-S	15.00	27.50	80,000
1860	7.50	8.50	805,400
1860-O	7.50	8.50	388,000
1860-S	14.00	27.50	56,000
1861	7.50	8.50	4,854,600
1861-S	14.00	25.00	96,000
1862	7.50	8.50	932,550
1862-S	19.00	30.00	67,000
1863	16.50	27.50	192,060
1864	22.50	35.00	94,070
1864-S	40.00	95.00	20,000
1865	19.00	35.00	59,300
1865-S	16.50	35.00	41,000

with motto

Date	Good	Fine	Amount Minted
1866	$ 25.00	$ 47.50	17,525
1866-S	15.00	32.50	28,000
1867	25.00	47.50	20,625
1867-S	12.50	32.50	48,000
1868	18.00	37.50	30,000
1868-S	12.50	27.50	96,000
1869	25.00	47.50	16,600
1869-S	9.50	27.50	76,000
1870	11.00	19.00	87,400
1870-CC	185.00	400.00	8,340
1871	8.50	11.00	171,232
1871-CC	110.00	275.00	10,890
1871-S	11.00	22.50	30,900
1872	8.50	11.00	182,950
1872-CC	160.00	330.00	9,100
1872-S	16.50	32.50	103,000
1873	7.50	10.00	220,600
1873 with arrows	13.50	25.00	1,263,700
1873-CC	4,000.00	7,500.00	4,000
1873-CC with arrows	145.00	350.00	12,462
1873-S with arrows	13.50	30.00	156,000
1874 with arrows	10.00	20.00	471,900
1874-S with arrows	14.00	30.00	392,000
1875	7.50	10.00	4,293,500
1875-CC	7.50	10.00	140,000
1875-S	7.50	10.00	680,000
1876	7.50	10.00	17,817,150
1876-CC	7.50	10.00	4,944,000
1876-S	7.50	10.00	8,596,000
1877	7.50	10.00	10,911,710
1877-CC	7.50	10.00	4,192,000
1877-S	7.50	10.00	8,996,000
1878	7.50	10.00	2,260,800
1878-CC	7.50	10.00	996,000
1878-S	65.00	130.00	140,000
1879	37.50	65.00	14,700
1880	37.50	65.00	14,955

1881	47.50	65.00	12,975
1882	47.50	65.00	16,300
1883	47.50	65.00	15,439
1884	50.00	70.00	8,875
1885	47.50	65.00	14,530
1886	60.00	100.00	5,886
1887	47.50	87.50	10,710
1888	47.50	87.50	10,833
1888-S	8.50	11.00	1,216,000
1889	37.50	60.00	12,711
1890	9.00	12.00	80,590
1891	7.50	10.00	3,920,600
1891-O	70.00	125.00	68,000
1891-S	7.50	10.00	2,216,000

LIBERTY HEAD

CONDITION: *Good:* Liberty outlined with some details visible; most lettering and date readable. *Fine:* Most details of design and word LIBERTY on headband visible; other lettering and date sharp.

MINT MARK: On reverse, below the eagle.

Date	*Good*	*Fine*	*Amount Minted*
1892	$ 3.00	$ 4.00	8,237,245
1892-O	3.00	5.00	2,640,000
1892-S	6.00	20.00	964,079

1893	3.00	3.00	5,444,815
1893-O	3.00	4.00	3,396,000
1893-S	3.50	6.50	1,454,535
1894	3.00	3.00	3,432,972
1894-O	3.00	4.00	2,852,000
1894-S	3.00	4.00	2,648,821
1895	3.00	3.00	4,440,880
1895-O	3.00	4.00	2,816,000
1895-S	3.00	5.00	1,764,681
1896	3.00	3.00	3,874,762
1896-O	3.00	10.00	1,484,000
1896-S	100.00	200.00	188,039
1897	3.00	3.00	8,140,731
1897-O	6.00	12.50	1,414,800
1897-S	9.50	12.50	542,229
1898	3.00	3.00	11,100,735
1898-O	3.00	4.25	1,868,000
1898-S	3.00	4.25	1,020,592
1899	3.00	3.00	12,624,846
1899-O	3.00	4.25	2,644,000
1899-S	4.00	8.00	708,000
1900	3.00	3.00	10,016,912
1900-O	3.00	6.50	3,416,000
1900-S	3.00	4.50	1,858,585
1901	3.00	3.00	8,892,813
1901-O	5.00	20.00	1,612,000
1901-S	250.00	400.00	72,664
1902	3.00	3.00	12,197,744
1902-O	3.00	5.00	4,748,000
1902-S	3.50	6.50	1,524,612
1903	3.00	3.00	9,670,064
1903-O	3.00	6.00	3,500,000
1903-S	3.00	8.00	1,036,000
1904	3.00	3.00	9,588,813
1904-O	4.00	9.00	2,456,000
1905	3.00	3.00	4,968,250
1905-O	3.00	8.00	1,230,000
1905-S	3.00	5.00	1,884,000
1906	3.00	3.00	3,656,435

1906-D	3.00	3.00	3,280,000
1906-O	3.00	3.00	2,056,000
1907	3.00	3.00	7,192,575
1907-D	3.00	3.00	2,484,000
1907-O	3.00	3.00	4,560,000
1907-S	3.00	4.00	1,360,000
1908	3.00	3.00	4,232,545
1908-D	3.00	3.00	5,788,000
1908-O	3.00	3.00	6,244,000
1908-S	4.50	6.50	784,000
1909	3.00	3.00	9,268,650
1909-D	3.00	3.00	5,114,000
1909-O	4.50	17.50	712,000
1909-S	3.00	3.00	1,348,000
1910	3.00	3.00	2,244,551
1910-D	3.00	3.00	1,500,000
1911	3.00	3.00	3,720,543
1911-D	3.00	4.00	933,600
1911-S	3.00	4.00	988,000
1912	3.00	3.00	4,400,700
1912-S	3.00	4.25	708,000
1913	5.75	12.00	484,613
1913-D	3.00	3.00	1,450,800
1913-S	100.00	200.00	40,000
1914	3.00	3.00	6,244,610
1914-D	3.00	3.00	3,046,000
1914-S	4.50	12.00	264,000
1915	3.00	3.00	3,480,450
1915-D	3.00	3.00	3,694,000
1915-S	3.00	4.00	704,000
1916	3.00	3.00	1,788,000
1916-D	3.00	3.00	6,540,800

LIBERTY STANDING

CONDITION: *Good:* Liberty outlined but most details worn; lettering and date readable. *Fine:* Most details of design visible; all lettering and date sharp.

MINT MARK: On obverse, to left and slightly above date.

Date	*Good*	*Fine*	*Amount Minted*
1916	$350.00	$500.00	52,000
1917	3.50	4.00	8,792,000
1917 with 3 stars below eagle	3.00	3.00	13,880,000
1917-D	4.00	3.50	1,509,200
1917-D with 3 stars below eagle	7.50	11.00	6,224,400
1917-S	4.00	6.00	1,952,000
1917-S with 3 stars below eagle	10.00	12.50	5,552,000
1918	3.00	4.00	14,240,000
1918-D	5.00	7.50	7,380,000
1918-S	3.00	4.00	11,072,000
1918-S with 8 over 7	225.00	450.00	
1919	4.00	5.00	11,324,000
1919-D	15.00	25.00	1,944,000
1919-S	15.00	25.00	1,836,000
1920	3.00	3.00	27,860,000
1920-D	7.50	12.50	3,586,400
1920-S	5.00	7.50	6,380,000
1921	15.00	25.00	1,916,000
1923	3.00	4.00	9,716,000

1923-S	20.00	30.00	1,360,000
1924	3.00	3.50	10,920,000
1924-D	5.00	10.00	3,112,000
1924-S	4.00	8.50	2,860,000
1925	3.00	3.50	12,280,000
1926	3.00	3.50	11,316,000
1926-D	3.00	3.50	1,716,000
1926-S	3.00	4.00	2,700,000
1927	3.00	3.50	11,912,000
1927-D	3.00	3.50	976,400
1927-S	4.00	5.00	396,000
1928	3.00	3.50	6,336,000
1928-D	3.00	3.50	1,627,600
1928-S	3.00	3.50	2,644,000
1929	3.00	3.50	11,140,000
1929-D	3.00	3.50	1,358,000
1929-S	3.00	3.50	1,764,000
1930	3.00	3.50	5,632,000
1930-S	3.00	3.50	1,556,000

WASHINGTON QUARTER DOLLAR

CONDITION: *V. Good:* Most details of Washington head visible; tips of eagle's wings outlined but feathers worn; all lettering and date readable. *V. Fine:* All details of design, lettering and date sharp; coin should show only slight signs of wear.

MINT MARK: 1932–64: On reverse, below the eagle; 1968 —: On obverse.

Date	V. Good	V. Fine	Amount Minted
1932	$ 1.25*	$ 1.50*	5,404,000
1932-D	28.00	45.00	436,800
1932-S	25.00	35.00	408,000
1934	1.25*	1.50*	31,912,052
1934-D	1.25*	1.50*	3,527,200
1935	1.25*	1.50*	32,484,000
1935-D	1.25*	1.50*	5,780,000
1935-S	1.25*	1.50*	5,660,000
1936	1.25*	1.50*	41,303,837
1936-D	1.25*	1.50*	5,374,000
1936-S	1.25*	1.50*	3,828,000
1937	1.25*	1.50*	19,701,542
1937-D	1.25*	1.50*	7,189,600
1937-S	3.00	4.00	1,652,000
1938	1.25*	1.50*	9,480,045
1938-S	1.25*	1.50*	2,832,000
1939	1.25*	1.50*	33,548,795
1939-D	1.25*	1.50*	7,092,000
1939-S	1.25*	1.50*	2,628,000
1940	1.25*	1.50*	35,715,246
1940-D	1.25*	1.50*	2,797,600
1940-S	1.25*	1.50*	8,244,000
1941	1.25*	1.50*	79,047,287
1941-D	1.25*	1.50*	16,714,800
1941-S	1.25*	1.50*	16,080,000
1942	1.25*	1.50*	102,117,123
1942-D	1.25*	1.50*	17,487,200
1942-S	1.25*	1.50*	19,384,000
1943	1.25*	1.50*	99,700,000
1943-D	1.25*	1.50*	16,095,600
1943-S	1.25*	1.50*	21,700,000
1944	1.25*	1.50*	104,956,000
1944-D	1.25*	1.50*	14,600,000
1944-S	1.25*	1.50*	12,560,000
1945	1.25*	1.50*	74,372,000
1945-D	1.25*	1.50*	12,341,600
1945-S	1.25*	1.50*	17,004,001

** Coins marked with an asterisk are discussed on pages 25-26.*

1946	1.25*	1.50*	53,436,000
1946-D	1.25*	1.50*	9,072,800
1946-S	1.25*	1.50*	4,204,000
1947	1.25*	1.50*	22,556,000
1947-D	1.25*	1.50*	15,338,400
1947-S	1.25*	1.50*	5,532,000
1948	1.25*	1.50*	35,196,000
1948-D	1.25*	1.50*	16,766,800
1948-S	1.25*	1.50*	15,960,000
1949	1.25*	1.50*	9,312,000
1949-D	1.25*	1.50*	10,068,400
1950	1.25*	1.50*	24,971,512
1950-D	1.25*	1.50*	21,075,600
1950-S	1.25*	1.50*	10,284,004
1951	1.25*	1.50*	43,505,602
1951-D	1.25*	1.50*	35,354,800
1951-S	1.25*	1.50*	8,948,000
1952	1.25*	1.50*	38,862,073
1952-D	1.25*	1.50*	49,795,200
1952-S	1.25*	1.50*	13,707,800
1953	1.25*	1.50*	18,664,920
1953-D	1.25*	1.50*	56,112,400
1953-S	1.25*	1.50*	14,016,000
1954	1.25*	1.50*	54,645,503
1954-D	1.25*	1.50*	46,305,500
1954-S	1.25*	1.50*	11,834,722
1955	1.25*	1.50*	18,558,831
1955-D	1.25*	1.50*	3,182,400
1956	1.25*	1.50*	44,813,384
1956-D	1.25*	1.50*	32,334,500
1957	1.25*	1.50*	47,779,852
1957-D	1.25*	1.50*	77,924,160
1958	1.25*	1.50*	7,235,652
1958-D	1.25*	1.50*	78,124,900
1959	1.25*	1.50*	25,533,291
1959-D	1.25*	1.50*	62,054,232
1960	1.25*	1.50*	30,855,602
1960-D	1.25*	1.50*	63,000,324
1961	1.25*	1.50*	37,036,000
1961-D	1.25*	1.50*	83,656,928

** Coins marked with an asterisk are discussed on pages 25-26.*

1962	1.25*	1.50*	39,374,019
1962-D	1.25*	1.50*	127,554,756
1963	1.25*	1.50*	74,316,000
1963-D	1.25*	1.50*	135,288,184
1964	1.25*	1.50*	559,700,482
1964-D	1.25*	1.50*	704,135,528
1965	.25	.25	1,819,717,540
1966	.25	.25	821,101,500
1967	.25	.25	1,524,031,848
1968	.25	.25	220,731,500
1968-D	.25	.25	101,534,000
1969	.25	.25	176,212,000
1969-D	.25	.25	114,372,000
1970	.25	.25	136,420,000
1970-D	.25	.25	417,341,364
1971	.25	.25	109,284,000
1971-D	.25	.25	258,634,428
1972	.25	.25	215,048,000
1972-D	.25	.25	311,067,732
1973-1982	.25	.25	—

* *Coins marked with an asterisk are discussed on pages 25-26.*

15

HALF DOLLARS

Half dollars were first struck in silver in 1794. Early coins of this denomination showed no value on the face of the coin, but the words FIFTY CENTS OR HALF A DOLLAR were stamped on the coin's edge. In 1807, the value "50 C." appeared on the coin's reverse. In 1836, the value was changed to read 50 CENTS and the lettered edge was replaced with a reeded edge. In 1838, the value was designated by the words HALF DOL. The early types of half dollars are: Liberty with Flowing Hair (1794–95); Liberty with Draped Bust (1796–1807); Liberty with Turban (1807–39); Liberty Seated (1839–91).

The Liberty Head half dollar, also called the "Barber" half dollar, after its designer, Charles E. Barber, was introduced in 1892. This was the first half dollar piece to carry the value HALF DOLLAR spelled out in full.

The Liberty Walking half dollar replaced the Liberty Head in 1916. This coin was designed by A. A. Weinman.

The Franklin half dollar was introduced in 1948. This coin, designed by John R. Sinnock, was discontinued after 1963.

In 1964, to honor the late president, the Kennedy half dollar was introduced. This coin was received very enthusiastically. Its obverse was designed by Gilroy Roberts; the reverse was designed by Frank Gasparro.

Note: *Prices for "common" silver half dollars are based on the price of silver. For details, see page* 26.

LIBERTY WITH FLOWING HAIR

CONDITION: *Good:* Liberty outlined but most details worn smooth; lettering and date readable. *Fine:* Most details of design visible; lettering and date sharp.

MINT MARK: None.

Date		*Good*	*Fine*	*Amount Minted*
1794		$500.00	$1,250.00	5,300
1795	with 2 leaves under eagle's wings	350.00	750.00	317,836 (both 1795 varieties)
1795	with 3 leaves under eagle's wings	450.00	1,000.00	

LIBERTY WITH DRAPED BUST

with small eagle

CONDITION: *Good:* Liberty outlined but most details worn smooth; lettering and date readable. *Fine:* Most details of design visible; lettering and date sharp.

MINT MARK: None.

Date	*Good*	*Fine*	*Amount Minted*
1796 with 15 stars	$4,500.00	$9,000.00	———
1796 with 16 stars	4,750.00	9,500.00	
1797	4,500.00	9,000.00	3,918

with large eagle

Date	*Good*	*Fine*	*Amount Minted*
1801	$135.00	$265.00	30,289
1802	100.00	250.00	29,890
1803	45.00	90.00	31,715
1805	40.00	70.00	211,722
1805 with 5 over 4	50.00	100.00	
1806	35.00	50.00	839,576
1806 with 6 over 5	45.00	70.00	
1806 with 6 over inverted 6	75.00	150.00	
1807	35.00	75.00	301,076

LIBERTY WITH TURBAN

with motto

CONDITION: *Good:* Liberty outlined but most details worn; lettering and date readable. *Fine:* Most details of design and word LIBERTY on headband visible; other lettering and date sharp.

MINT MARK: On reverse, below the eagle.

Date	*Good*	*Fine*	*Amount Minted*
1807	$ 15.00	$ 35.00	750,500
1808	12.50	17.50	1,368,600
1808 with 08 over 07	15.00	25.00	
1809	12.50	17.50	1,405,810
1810	12.50	17.50	1,276,276
1811	12.50	17.50	1,203,644
1812	12.50	17.50	1,628,059
1812 with 2 over 1	15.00	20.00	
1813	12.50	17.50	1,241,903
1814	12.50	17.50	1,039,075
1814 with 4 over 3	16.50	25.00	
1815 with 5 over 2	250.00	400.00	47,150
1817	12.50	17.50	1,215,567
1817 dated 181.7	15.00	27.50	
1817 with 7 over 3	15.00	27.50	1,960,322
1818	12.50	17.50	
1818 with 18 over 17	13.50	20.00	

1819	11.50	17.50	2,208,000
1819 with 19 over 18	11.50	17.50	
1820	20.00	30.00	751,122
1820 with 20 over 19	20.00	30.00	
1821	11.50	17.50	1,305,797
1822	11.50	17.50	1,559,573
1822 with 22 over 21	35.00	80.00	
1823	11.50	17.50	1,694,200
1824	11.50	17.50	3,504,954
1824 with 4 over 1	12.50	20.00	
1824 over other dates	12.50	20.00	
1825	11.50	17.50	2,943,166
1826	11.50	17.50	4,004,180
1827	11.50	17.50	5,493,400
1827 with 7 over 6	17.50	25.00	
1828	11.50	17.50	3,075,200
1828 with curled base, knobbed 2	35.00	55.00	
1829	11.50	17.50	3,712,256
1829 with 9 over 7	13.50	20.00	
1830	11.50	17.50	4,764,800
1831	11.50	17.50	5,837,660
1832	11.50	17.50	4,797,000
1833	11.50	17.50	5,206,000
1834	11.50	17.50	6,412,004
1835	11.50	17.50	5,352,006
1836 with lettered edge	11.50	17.50	6,546,200

without motto

Date	*Good*	*Fine*	*Amount Minted*
1836 with reeded edge	$225.00	$490.00	included above
1837	17.50	25.00	3,629,820
1838	17.50	25.00	3,546,000
1839-O	70.00	150.00	162,976
1839	17.50	25.00	3,334,560

	Proof	
1838-O	$35,000.00	20

LIBERTY SEATED

with arrows at date *with rays around eagle*

CONDITION: *Good:* Liberty outlined but most details worn; lettering and date readable. *Fine:* Details and LIBERTY on shield visible; other lettering and date readable.

MINT MARK: On reverse, below the eagle.

Date	*Good*	*Fine*	*Amount Minted*
1839	$10.00	$ 15.00	included above
1840	10.00	15.00	1,435,008
1840-O	10.00	15.00	855,100
1841	11.50	17.50	310,000
1841-O	10.00	15.00	401,000
1842	10.00	15.00	2,012,764
1842-O with large date	10.00	15.00	957,000
1842-O with small date	55.00	120.00	
1843	10.00	15.00	3,844,000
1843-O	10.00	15.00	2,268,000
1844	10.00	15.00	1,766,000
1844-O	10.00	15.00	2,005,000
1845	13.50	20.00	589,000
1845-O	10.00	15.00	2,094,000
1846	10.00	15.00	2,210,000
1846 with 6 over horizontal 6	45.00	90.00	
1846-O	10.00	15.00	2,304,000
1847	10.00	15.00	1,156,000
1847-O	10.00	15.00	2,584,000
1848	20.00	30.00	580,000
1848-O	10.00	15.00	3,180,000
1849	10.00	15.00	1,252,000
1849-O	10.00	15.00	2,310,000
1850	25.00	40.00	227,000
1850-O	10.00	15.00	2,456,000
1851	30.00	50.00	200,750
1851-O	10.00	15.00	402,000
1852	35.00	55.00	77,130
1852-O	20.00	32.50	144,000
1853 with arrows and rays	10.00	15.00	3,532,708
1853-O with arrows and rays	10.00	15.00	1,328,000
1854 with arrows	10.00	15.00	2,982,000

1854-O with arrows	10.00	15.00	5,240,000
1855 with arrows	10.00	15.00	759,500
1855-O with arrows	10.00	15.00	3,688,000
1855-S with arrows	50.00	115.00	129,950
1856	10.00	15.00	938,000
1856-O	10.00	15.00	2,658,000
1856-S	15.00	27.50	211,000
1857	10.00	15.00	1,988,000
1857-O	10.00	15.00	818,000
1857-S	20.00	27.50	158,000
1858	10.00	15.00	4,226,000
1858-O	10.00	15.00	7,294,000
1858-S	13.50	20.00	476,000
1859	10.00	15.00	748,000
1859-O	10.00	15.00	2,834,000
1859-S	10.00	15.00	566,000
1860	10.00	15.00	303,700
1860-O	10.00	15.00	1,290,000
1860-S	10.00	15.00	472,000
1861	10.00	15.00	2,888,400
1861 Confederate restrike	240.00	360.00	——
1861-O	10.00	15.00	330,000
1861-S	10.00	15.00	939,500
1862	12.50	22.50	252,350
1862-S	10.00	15.00	1,352,000
1863	10.00	15.00	503,660
1863-S	10.00	15.00	916,000
1864	12.50	22.50	379,570
1864-S	10.00	15.00	658,000
1865	10.00	15.00	511,900
1865-S	10.00	15.00	675,000
1866-S	32.50	65.00	1,054,000

with motto

Date	*Good*	*Fine*	*Amount Minted*
1866	$ 10.00	$ 15.00	745,625
1866-S	10.00	15.00	———
1867	10.00	15.00	424,325
1867-S	10.00	15.00	1,196,000
1868	12.50	20.00	378,200
1868-S	10.00	15.00	1,160,000
1869	10.00	15.00	795,900
1869-S	10.00	15.00	656,000
1870	10.00	15.00	600,900
1870-CC	115.00	375.00	54,617
1870-S	10.00	15.00	1,004,000
1871	10.00	15.00	1,165,360
1871-CC	35.00	70.00	139,950
1871-S	10.00	15.00	2,178,000
1872	10.00	15.00	881,550
1872-CC	30.00	65.00	272,000
1872-S	10.00	15.00	580,000
1873	10.00	15.00	801,800
1873 with arrows	14.00	25.00	1,815,700
1873-CC	45.00	90.00	122,500
1873-CC with arrows	22.50	45.00	214,560
1873-S with arrows	15.00	30.00	228,000
1874 with arrows	15.00	25.00	2,360,300
1874-CC with arrows	30.00	90.00	59,000
1874-S with arrows	15.00	30.00	394,000
1875	10.00	15.00	6,027,500
1875-CC	11.00	17.50	1,008,000

1875-S	10.00	15.00	3,200,000
1876	10.00	15.00	8,419,150
1876-CC	10.00	15.00	1,956,000
1876-S	10.00	15.00	4,528,000
1877	10.00	15.00	8,304,510
1877-CC	10.00	15.00	1,420,000
1877-S	10.00	15.00	5,356,000
1878	10.00	15.00	1,378,400
1878-CC	135.00	225.00	62,000
1878-S	950.00	2,000.00	12,000
1879	80.00	125.00	5,900
1880	80.00	125.00	9,755
1881	80.00	125.00	10,975
1882	80.00	125.00	5,500
1883	80.00	125.00	9,039
1884	80.00	125.00	5,275
1885	80.00	125.00	6,130
1886	80.00	125.00	5,886
1887	80.00	125.00	5,710
1888	80.00	125.00	12,833
1889	80.00	125.00	12,711
1890	80.00	125.00	12,590
1891	20.00	25.00	200,600

LIBERTY HEAD

CONDITION: *Good:* Liberty outlined with some details visible; most lettering and date readable. *Fine:* Most details of design and word LIBERTY on headband readable; other lettering and date sharp.

MINT MARK: On reverse, below the eagle.

Date	*Good*	*Fine*	*Amount Minted*
1892	$ 4.00	$10.00	935,245
1892-O	16.50	30.00	390,000
1892-S	16.50	27.50	1,029,028
1893	4.00	10.00	1,826,792
1893-O	4.00	10.00	1,389,000
1893-S	13.50	23.00	740,000
1894	4.00	10.00	1,148,972
1894-O	4.00	10.00	2,138,000
1894-S	4.00	10.00	4,048,690
1895	4.00	10.00	1,835,218
1895-O	4.00	10.00	1,766,000
1895-S	4.00	10.00	1,108,086
1896	4.00	10.00	950,762
1896-O	7.00	10.00	924,000
1896-S	13.50	30.00	1,140,948
1897	4.00	10.00	2,480,731
1897-O	14.50	32.50	632,000
1897-S	14.50	32.50	933,900
1898	4.00	10.00	2,956,735
1898-O	4.00	10.00	874,000
1898-S	4.00	10.00	2,358,550
1899	4.00	10.00	5,538,846
1899-O	4.00	10.00	1,724,000
1899-S	4.00	10.00	1,686,411
1900	4.00	10.00	4,762,912
1900-O	4.00	10.00	2,744,000
1900-S	4.00	10.00	2,560,322
1901	4.00	10.00	4,268,813
1901-O	4.00	10.00	1,124,000
1901-S	8.00	30.00	847,044
1902	4.00	10.00	4,922,777
1902-O	4.00	10.00	2,526,000
1902-S	4.00	10.00	1,460,670
1903	4.00	10.00	2,278,755
1903-O	4.00	10.00	2,100,000

1903-S	4.00	10.00	1,920,772
1904	4.00	10.00	2,992,670
1904-O	4.00	10.00	1,117,600
1904-S	4.00	16.00	553,038
1905	4.00	15.00	662,727
1905-O	4.00	14.00	505,000
1905-S	4.00	10.00	2,494,000
1906	4.00	10.00	2,638,675
1906-D	4.00	10.00	4,028,000
1906-O	4.00	10.00	2,446,000
1906-S	4.00	10.00	1,740,154
1907	4.00	10.00	2,598,575
1907-D	4.00	10.00	3,856,000
1907-O	4.00	10.00	3,946,600
1907-S	4.00	10.00	1,250,000
1908	4.00	10.00	1,354,545
1908-D	4.00	10.00	3,280,000
1908-O	4.00	10.00	5,360,000
1908-S	4.00	10.00	1,644,828
1909	4.00	10.00	2,368,650
1909-O	4.00	12.50	925,400
1909-S	4.00	10.00	1,764,000
1910	4.00	12.50	418,551
1910-S	4.00	10.00	1,948,000
1911	4.00	10.00	1,406,543
1911-D	4.00	10.00	695,080
1911-S	4.00	10.00	1,272,000
1912	4.00	10.00	1,550,700
1912-D	4.00	10.00	2,300,800
1912-S	4.00	10.00	1,370,000
1913	4.00	12.50	188,627
1913-D	4.00	10.00	534,000
1913-S	4.00	10.00	604,000
1914	4.00	14.50	124,610
1914-S	4.00	10.00	992,000
1915	4.00	14.50	138,450
1915-D	4.00	10.00	1,170,400
1915-S	4.00	10.00	1,604,000

LIBERTY WALKING

CONDITION: *V. Good:* Most details of design visible; all lettering and date sharp. *V. Fine:* All details of design, lettering and date sharp; coin should show only slight signs of wear.

MINT MARK: 1916–17: On obverse, below the motto; 1917–47: On reverse, to left of value.

Date	*V. Good*	*V. Fine*	*Amount Minted*
1916	$ 2.50	$ 3.00	608,000
1916-D	2.50	3.00	1,014,400
1916-S	10.00	17.50	508,000
1917	2.50	3.00	12,292,000
1917-D with D on obverse	2.50	3.00	765,400
1917-D with D on reverse	2.50	3.00	1,940,000
1917-S with S on obverse	2.50	15.00	952,000
1917-S with S on reverse	2.50	3.00	5,554,000
1918	2.50	3.00	6,634,000
1918-D	2.50	3.00	3,853,040
1918-S	2.50	3.00	10,282,000
1919	2.50	3.00	962,000
1919-D	2.50	3.00	1,165,000
1919-S	2.50	10.00	1,552,000
1920	2.50	3.00	6,372,000

1920-D	2.50	3.00	1,551,000
1920-S	2.50	3.00	4,624,000
1921	15.00	35.00	246,000
1921-D	25.00	45.00	208,000
1921-S	2.50	7.50	548,000
1923-S	2.50	3.00	2,178,000
1927-S	2.50	3.00	2,392,000
1928-S	2.50	3.00	1,940,000
1929-D	2.50	3.00	1,001,200
1929-S	2.50	3.00	1,902,000
1933-S	2.50	3.00	1,786,000
1934	2.50	3.00	6,964,000
1934-D	2.50	3.00	2,361,400
1934-S	2.50	3.00	3,652,000
1935	2.50	3.00	9,162,000
1935-D	2.50	3.00	3,003,800
1935-S	2.50	3.00	3,854,000
1936	2.50	3.00	12,617,901
1936-D	2.50	3.00	4,252,400
1936-S	2.50	3.00	3,884,000
1937	2.50	3.00	9,527,728
1937-D	2.50	3.00	1,760,001
1937-S	2.50	3.00	2,090,000
1938	2.50	3.00	4,118,152
1938-D	12.50	17.50	491,600
1939	2.50	3.00	6,820,808
1939-D	2.50	3.00	4,267,800
1939-S	2.50	3.00	2,552,000
1940	2.50	3.00	9,167,279
1940-S	2.50	3.00	4,550,000
1941	2.50	3.00	24,207,412
1941-D	2.50	3.00	11.248,400
1941-S	2.50	3.00	8,098,000
1942	2.50	3.00	14,839,120
1942-D	2.50	3.00	10,973,800
1942-S	2.50	3.00	12,708,000
1943	2.50	3.00	53,190,000
1943-D	2.50	3.00	11,346,000
1943-S	2.50	3.00	13,450,000

1944	2.50	3.00	28,206,000
1944-D	2.50	3.00	9,769,000
1944-S	2.50	3.00	8,904,000
1945	2.50	3.00	31,502,000
1945-D	2.50	3.00	9,966,800
1945-S	2.50	3.00	10,156,000
1946	2.50	3.00	12,118,000
1946-D	2.50	3.00	2,151,100
1946-S	2.50	3.00	3,724,000
1947	2.50	3.00	4,094,000
1947-D	2.50	3.00	3,900,600

FRANKLIN HALF DOLLAR

CONDITION: *Ex. Fine:* All details of design, lettering and date sharp; coin should show only slight signs of wear.

MINT MARK: On reverse, above Liberty Bell.

Date	*Ex. Fine*	*Amount Minted*
1948	$2.50	3,006,814
1948-D	2.50	4,028,600
1949	2.50	5,714,000
1949-D	2.50	4,120,600
1949-S	2.50	3,744,000
1950	2.50	7,793,509
1950-D	2.50	8,031,600

1951	2.50	16,859,602
1951-D	2.50	9,475,200
1951-S	2.50	13,696,000
1952	2.50	21,274,073
1952-D	2.50	25,395,600
1952-S	2.50	5,526,000
1953	2.50	2,796,920
1953-D	2.50	20,900,400
1953-S	2.50	4,148,000
1954	2.50	13,421,503
1954-D	2.50	25,445,580
1954-S	2.50	4,993,400
1955	2.50	2,876,381
1956	2.50	4,701,384
1957	2.50	6,361,952
1957-D	2.50	19,966,850
1958	2.50	4,917,652
1958-D	2.50	23,962,412
1959	2.50	7,349,291
1959-D	2.50	13,053,750
1960	2.50	7,715,602
1960-D	2.50	18,215,812
1961	2.50	8,290,000
1961-D	2.50	20,276,442
1962	2.50	12,932,019
1962-D	2.50	35,473,281
1963	2.50	22,164,000
1964-D	2.50	67,059,292

KENNEDY HALF DOLLAR

CONDITION: *Ex. Fine:* All details of design, lettering and date sharp; coin should show only slight signs of wear.

MINT MARK: 1964: On reverse, below and to left of eagle; 1968—: On obverse.

Date	*Ex. Fine*	*Amount Minted*
1964	$ 2.50	235,580,766
1964-D	2.50	156,205,446
1965	1.00	65,879,366
1966	1.00	108,984,932
1967	1.00	295,046,978
1968-D	1.00	246,951,930
1969-D	1.00	129,881,800
1970-D	15.00	2,150,000
1971	.50	155,164,000
1971-D	.50	302,097,424
1972	.50	153,180,000
1972-D	.50	141,890,000
1973-1982	.50	———

16

SILVER DOLLARS

Silver dollars were struck from 1794 to 1935. Early silver dollars did not show a face value on the coin itself, but the words HUNDRED CENTS, ONE DOLLAR OR UNIT were stamped on the coin's edge. In 1840, the value appeared on the reverse of the coin with the words ONE DOL. At the same time, the lettered edge was replaced with a reeded edge.

Early types of silver dollars are: Liberty with Flowing Hair (1794–95); Liberty with Draped Bust (1795–1804); Liberty Seated (1840–73).

While no silver dollars were officially issued from 1805 through 1839, Christian Gobrecht designed a pattern coin that was struck in 1836, 1838 and 1839; these coins are quite rare. The obverse of the Gobrecht dollar shows Liberty Seated. This design was used when coinage of silver dollars resumed in 1840 and for all silver coins of the period. The reverse of the Gobrecht dollar shows a graceful eagle in flight, a design that was later adopted for use on the obverse of the Flying Eagle cent.

Another silver dollar that was not actually intended for general circulation in this country was the Trade dollar, struck from 1873 to 1885. This coin was issued to compete with the Mexican *peso* in our trade with the Orient (trade that had fallen off considerably during the Civil

War). This coin contained a higher quantity of silver than other silver dollars and during its first years of issue was considered legal tender in this country for amounts up to $5.00. When the price of silver declined, the coin was limited solely to circulation in the Orient.

In 1878, the Liberty Head (or "Morgan") dollar was introduced. This coin, designed by George T. Morgan, was minted in very large quantities until 1904. Under provisions of the Pittman Act, this coin was reissued again for the year 1921.

During the same year, 1921, the Peace dollar was introduced. This coin, designed by Anthony de Francisci, was issued to commemorate the end of World War I. The Peace dollar was minted until 1935, when the coin was discontinued.

LIBERTY WITH FLOWING HAIR

CONDITION: *Good:* Liberty outlined but most details worn smooth; lettering and date readable. *Fine:* Most details of hair and feathers visible; lettering and date sharp.

MINT MARK: None.

Date	*Good*	*Fine*	*Amount Minted*
1794	$3,000.00	$7,500.00	1,758
1795	600.00	1,200.00	184,013

LIBERTY WITH DRAPED BUST

with small eagle

CONDITION: *Good:* Liberty outlined but most details worn smooth; lettering and date clear. *Fine:* Most details of hair, drapery and feathers visible; lettering and date sharp. *Proof:* Coin should be in unused condition.

MINT MARK: None.

Date	*Good*	*Fine*	*Amount Minted*
1795	$440.00	$850.00	included above
1796	440.00	850.00	72,920
1797	440.00	850.00	7,776
1798	440.00	850.00	327,536

with large eagle

Date	*Good*	*Fine*	*Amount Minted*
1798	$255.00	$325.00	included above
1799	255.00	325.00	423,515
1800	255.00	325.00	220,920
1801	255.00	325.00	54,454
1802	255.00	325.00	41,650
1803	255.00	325.00	6,064

	Proof	
1804	$100,000.00	———

GOBRECHT DOLLAR

CONDITION: *Proof:* Coin should be in unused condition.

MINT MARK: None.

Date	Proof	Amount Minted
1836	$ 4,000.00	1,000
1838	8,000.00	———
1839	6,500.00	300

LIBERTY SEATED

without motto

CONDITION: *V. Good:* Most details of design visible; word LIBERTY on shield worn but readable; other lettering and date sharp. *V. Fine:* All details of design, lettering and date sharp. *Proof:* Coin should be in unused condition with mirror surface.

MINT MARK: On reverse, below the eagle.

Date	V. Good	V. Fine	Amount Minted
1840	$ 55.00	$ 85.00	61,005
1841	42.50	80.00	173,000
1842	42.50	80.00	184,618
1843	42.50	80.00	165,100
1844	100.00	135.00	20,000

1845	100.00	125.00	24,500
1846	45.00	57.50	110,600
1846-O	55.00	62.50	59,000
1847	45.00	57.50	140,750
1848	85.00	115.00	15,000
1849	45.00	57.50	62,600
1850	120.00	145.00	7,500
1850-O	55.00	100.00	40,000
1853	100.00	140.00	46,110
1854	120.00	205.00	33,140
1855	130.00	225.00	26,000
1856	77.50	110.00	63,500
1857	77.50	110.00	94,000
1859	45.00	85.00	256,500
1859-0	45.00	57.50	360,000
1859-S	72.50	120.00	20,000
1860	42.50	57.50	218,930
1860-O	45.00	57.50	515,000
1861	75.00	100.00	78,500
1862	100.00	125.00	12,090
1863	85.00	110.00	27,660
1864	85.00	110.00	31,170
1865	85.00	110.00	47,000

	Proof	
1851	$6,500.00	1,300
1852	6,500.00	1,100
1858	4,800.00	——

with motto

Date	V. Good	V. Fine	Amount Minted
1866	$ 55.00	$ 100.00	49,625
1867	55.00	100.00	60,325
1868	45.00	60.00	182,700
1869	45.00	60.00	424,300
1870	42.50	55.00	433,000
1870-CC	100.00	200.00	12,462
1870-S	15,000.00	25,000.00	———
1871	42.50	55.00	1,115,760
1871-CC	500.00	775.00	3,150
1872	42.50	55.00	1,106,450
1872-CC	300.00	425.00	3,150
1872-S	55.00	115.00	9,000
1873	47.50	55.00	293,600
1873-CC	600.00	1,000.00	2,300

LIBERTY HEAD

CONDITION: *Ex. Fine:* All details of design, lettering and date sharp; coin should show only slight signs of wear.

MINT MARK: On reverse, below the eagle.

Date	*Ex. Fine*	*Amount Minted*
1878 with 7 tail feathers	$ 10.00	10,509,550
1878 with 8 tail feathers	10.00	
1877-CC	10.00	2,212,000
1878-S	10.00	9,774,000
1879	10.00	14,807,100
1879-CC	42.50	756,000
1879-O	10.00	2,887,000
1879-S	10.00	9,110,000
1880	10.00	12,601,355
1880-CC	27.50	591,000
1880-O	10.00	5,305,000
1880-S	10.00	8,900,000
1881	10.00	9,163,975
1881-CC	35.00	296,000
1880-O	10.00	5,708,000
1881-S	10.00	12,760,000
1882	10.00	11,101,100
1882-CC	10.00	1,133,000
1882-O	10.00	6,090,000
1882-S	10.00	9,250,000
1883	10.00	12,291,039
1883-CC	10.00	1,204,000
1883-O	10.00	8,725,000
1883-S	10.00	6,250,000
1884	10.00	14,070,875
1884-CC	22.50	1,136,000
1884-O	10.00	9,730,000
1884-S	10.00	3,200,000
1885	10.00	17,787,767
1885-CC	42.50	228,000
1885-O	10.00	9,185,000
1885-S	10.00	1,497,000
1886	10.00	19,963,886
1886-O	10.00	10,710,000
1886-S	10.00	750,000
1887	10.00	20,290,710

1887-O	10.00	11,550,000
1887-S	10.00	1,771,000
1888	10.00	19,183,833
1888-O	10.00	12,150,000
1888-S	17.50	657,000
1889	10.00	21,726,811
1889-CC	77.50	350,000
1889-O	10.00	11,875,000
1889-S	15.00	700,000
1890	10.00	16,802,590
1890-CC	10.00	2,309,041
1890-O	10.00	10,701,000
1890-S	10.00	8,230,373
1891	10.00	8,694,206
1891-CC	10.00	1,618,000
1891-O	10.00	7,954,529
1891-S	10.00	5,296,000
1892	10.00	1,037,245
1892-CC	17.50	1,352,000
1892-O	10.00	2,744,000
1892-S	10.00	1,200,000
1893	10.00	378,792
1893-CC	35.00	677,000
1893-O	20.00	300,000
1893-S	360.00	100,000
1894	47.50	110,972
1894-O	10.00	1,723,000
1894-S	10.00	1,260,000
1895-O	17.50	450,000
1895-S	35.00	400,000
1896	10.00	9,976,762
1896-O	10.00	4,900,000
1896-S	10.00	5,000,000
1897	10.00	2,822,731
1897-O	10.00	4,004,000
1897-S	10.00	5,825,000
1898	10.00	5,884,735
1898-O	10.00	4,440,000
1898-S	10.00	4,102,000

1899	10.00	330,846
1899-O	10.00	12,290,000
1899-S	10.00	2,562,000
1900	10.00	8,830,912
1900-O	10.00	12,590,000
1900-S	10.00	3,540,000
1901	10.00	6,962,813
1901-O	10.00	13,320,000
1901-S	10.00	2,284,000
1902	10.00	7,994,777
1902-O	10.00	8,636,000
1902-S	10.00	1,530,000
1903	10.00	4,652,755
1903-O	10.00	4,450,000
1903-S	10.00	1,241,000
1904	10.00	2,788,650
1904-O	10.00	3,720,000
1904-S	10.00	2,304,000
1921	10.00	44,690,000
1921-D	10.00	20,345,000
1921-S	10.00	21,695,000

Proof

1895	$10,000.00	12,880

PEACE DOLLAR

CONDITION: *Ex. Fine:* All details of design, lettering and date sharp; coin should show only slight signs of wear.

MINT MARK: On reverse, lower left of eagle's wing.

Date	*Ex. Fine*	*Amount Minted*
1921	$ 15.00	1,006,473
1922	10.00	51,737,000
1922-D	10.00	15,063,000
1922-S	10.00	17,475,000
1923	10.00	30,800,000
1923-D	10.00	6,811,000
1923-S	10.00	19,020,000
1924	10.00	11,811,000
1924-S	10.00	1,728,000
1925	10.00	10,198,000
1925-S	10.00	1,610,000
1926	10.00	1,939,000
1926-D	10.00	2,348,700
1926-S	10.00	6,980,000
1927	15.00	848,000
1927-D	10.00	1,268,900
1927-S	10.00	866,000
1928	42.50	360,649
1928-S	10.00	1,632,000
1934	10.00	954,057
1934-D	10.00	1,569,500
1934-S	10.00	1,011,000
1935	10.00	1,576,000
1935-S	10.00	1,964,000

TRADE DOLLAR

CONDITION: *V. Good:* Most details of design visible; word LIBERTY on banner and mottos worn but readable; other lettering and date sharp. *V. Fine:* All details of design, letter and date sharp.

MINT MARK: On reverse, below the eagle.

Date	*V. Good*	*V. Fine*	*Amount Minted*
1873	$ 35.00	$ 45.00	397,500
1873-CC	32.50	72.50	124,500
1873-S	32.50	45.00	703,000
1874	32.50	45.00	987,800
1874-CC	40.00	50.00	1,373,200
1874-S	32.50	45.00	2,549,000
1875	60.00	90.00	218,900
1875-CC	32.50	47.50	1,573,700
1875-S	32.50	45.00	4,487,000
1876	32.50	45.00	456,150
1876-CC	32.50	45.00	509,000
1876-S	32.50	45.00	5,227,000
1877	32.50	45.00	3,039,710
1877-CC	40.00	95.00	534,000
1877-S	32.50	45.00	9,519,000
1878-CC	85.00	180.00	97,000
1878-S	32.50	45.00	4,162,000

	Proof	*Amount Minted*
1878	$ 2,100.00	900
1879	1,700.00	1,541
1880	1,700.00	1,987
1881	1,700.00	960
1882	1,700.00	1,097
1883	1,700.00	979
1884	25,000.00	10
1885	50,000.00	5

17

PROOF SETS

A proof set consists of a cent, nickel, dime, quarter and half dollar, all struck in the same year—and all, of course, in proof condition (see Chapter 1). Until 1968, United States proof sets were struck only at the Philadelphia Mint, and were issued for the first time in 1936. They were issued yearly from 1936 through 1942, discontinued from 1943 through 1949, then issued again from 1950 through 1964, discontinued from 1965 to 1967, then issued again—struck at the San Francisco Mint from 1968 to the present.

Date	*Proof Set*	*Amount Minted*
1936	$ 4,000.00	3,837
1937	2,400.00	5,542
1938	1,050.00	8,045
1939	775.00	8,795
1940	650.00	11,246
1941	650.00	15,287
1942	650.00	21,120
1950	300.00	51,386
1951	200.00	57,500
1952	110.00	81,980
1953	75.00	128,800
1954	32.50	233,300
1955	32.50	378,200
1956	20.00	669,384

1957	11.00	1,247,952
1958	16.50	875,652
1959	11.00	1,149,291
1960	11.00	1,691,602
1961	11.00	3,028,244
1962	11.00	3,218,019
1963	11.00	3,075,645
1964	11.00	3,950,762
1968-S	4.00	3,041,509
1969-S	4.00	2,934,631
1970-S	6.00	2,632,810
1971-S	4.00	3,224,138
1972-S	4.00	3,267,667
1973-S	6.00	2,760,339
1974-S	6.00	———
1975-S	9.00	———

18

GOLD COINS

Gold, one of the most beautiful and precious metals known to man, is also very malleable, rust-proof, and tarnish-proof, making it an ideal material for coins. However, because of its natural softness, it must be alloyed when used for coinage so that it will be able to stand up under the abuse of normal circulation. The usual composition is nine parts gold to one part copper.

U. S. gold coins were struck from 1795 to 1933. In 1933, a presidential order discontinued issuance of all gold coins. By a recent Act, all U. S. gold coins have been determined to be collectors' items.

U. S. gold coins were issued in the following denominations: one dollar, quarter eagles ($2.50), three dollars, four dollars, half eagles ($5.00), eagles ($10.00) and double eagles ($20.00).

Note: *Prices for "common" gold coins are based largely on the world price of gold. For details,* *see page 26.*

19

GOLD DOLLARS

Gold dollars were struck from 1849 to 1889. They came into being with the discovery of gold in California. Prior to this discovery, gold was too scarce in this country to permit the issuance of so low a denomination.

Two basic types of gold dollars were issued: Liberty with Coronet (1849–54) and Liberty with Feather Headdress (1854–89). The former was the smallest coin ever struck at the U. S. Mint for general circulation. With the latter, the diameter of the coin was increased, but made thinner; hence, the weight of the coin remained unchanged.

LIBERTY WITH CORONET

CONDITION: *Fine:* Liberty outlined, with most details of hair and beads visible; word LIBERTY on crown worn but readable; other lettering and date sharp. *Ex. Fine:* All details of design, lettering and date sharp; coin should show only slight signs of wear.

MINT MARK: On reverse, below the wreath.

Date	*Fine*	*Ex. Fine*	*Amount Minted*
1849	$110.00	$170.00	688,567
1849-C	220.00	250.00	11,634
1849-D	210.00	325.00	21,588
1849-O	110.00	170.00	215,000
1850	110.00	170.00	481,953
1850-C	290.00	430.00	6,966
1850-D	290.00	430.00	8,382
1850-O	110.00	170.00	14,000
1851	110.00	170.00	3,317,671
1851-C	170.00	280.00	41,267
1851-D	225.00	535.00	9,882
1851-O	110.00	170.00	290,000
1852	110.00	170.00	2,045,351
1852-C	210.00	350.00	9,434
1853-D	210.00	430.00	6,360
1852-O	110.00	170.00	140,000
1853	110.00	170.00	4,076,051
1853-C	185.00	265.00	11,515
1853-D	325.00	535.00	6,583
1853-O	110.00	170.00	290,000
1854	110.00	170.00	1,639,445
1854-D	470.00	750.00	2,935
1854-S	120.00	210.00	14,632

See page 26 regarding prices listed for gold coins.

LIBERTY WITH FEATHER HEADDRESS

small Liberty

CONDITION: *Fine:* Liberty outlined; tips of feathers worn

but most other details of design visible; all lettering and date sharp: *Ex. Fine:* All details of design, lettering and date sharp; coin should show only slight signs of wear.

MINT MARK: On reverse, below the wreath.

Date	Fine	Ex. Fine	Amount Minted
1854	$ 165.00	$ 350.00	included in 1854 above
1855	165.00	350.00	758,269
1855-C	400.00	750.00	9,803
1855-D	1,750.00	3,750.00	1,811
1855-O	195.00	365.00	55,000
1856-S	195.00	365.00	24,600

large Liberty

Date	Fine	Ex. Fine	Amount Minted
1856	$ 110.00	$ 165.00	1,762,936
1856-D	1,250.00	2,750.00	1,460
1857	110.00	165.00	774,789
1857-C	200.00	300.00	13,280
1857-D	400.00	750.00	3,533
1857-S	110.00	165.00	10,000
1858	110.00	165.00	117,995
1858-D	400.00	750.00	3,477
1858-S	110.00	165.00	10,000
1859	110.00	165.00	168,244
1859-C	300.00	500.00	5,235
1859-D	300.00	600.00	4,952
1859-S	110.00	165.00	15,000

See page 26 regarding prices listed for gold coins.

1860	110.00	165.00	36,668
1860-D	1,500.00	3,250.00	1,566
1860-S	110.00	165.00	13,000
1861	110.00	165.00	527,499
1861-D	5,500.00	8,500.00	———
1862	110.00	165.00	1,326,865
1863	420.00	650.00	6,250
1864	230.00	490.00	5,950
1865	365.00	560.00	3,725
1866	230.00	350.00	7,180
1867	200.00	350.00	5,250
1868	200.00	350.00	10,525
1869	245.00	420.00	5,925
1870	200.00	325.00	6,335
1870-S	630.00	1,025.00	3,000
1871	200.00	325.00	3,930
1872	200.00	325.00	3,530
1873	200.00	325.00	125,125
1874	200.00	325.00	198,820
1875	2,250.00	3,850.00	420
1876	200.00	325.00	3,245
1877	200.00	325.00	3,920
1878	200.00	325.00	3,020
1879	200.00	325.00	3,030
1880	210.00	350.00	1,636
1881	200.00	325.00	7,660
1882	200.00	325.00	5,040
1883	200.00	325.00	10,840
1884	200.00	325.00	6,206
1885	200.00	325.00	12,205
1886	200.00	325.00	6,016
1887	200.00	325.00	8,543
1888	200.00	325.00	16,080
1889	200.00	325.00	30,729

See page 26 regarding prices listed for gold coins.

20

QUARTER EAGLES

($2.50)

Quarter eagles were struck from 1796 to 1929. The value did not appear on the face of the coin until 1808 when "2½ D." was added to the reverse. In 1908, the word DOLLARS was spelled out.

The following types of quarter eagles were issued: Liberty Head (1796–1807); Liberty with Turban (1808–34); Liberty with Ribbon (1834–39); Liberty with Coronet (1840–1907); Indian Head (1908–29).

In 1848, a shipment of gold from California was used to strike quarter eagles; such coins have the abbreviation CAL. stamped on the reverse, above the eagle.

The Indian Head quarter eagle and its half eagle counterpart are the only U. S. coins with an incuse design (a design sunk into the coin, rather than raised). The designer of these coins was Bela Lyon Pratt.

LIBERTY HEAD

without stars *with stars*

CONDITION: *Fine:* Liberty outlined with most details of design visible; E PLURIBUS UNUM worn but readable; other lettering and date sharp. *Ex. Fine:* All details, lettering and date sharp; coin should show only slight signs of wear.

MINT MARK: None.

Date	*Fine*	*Ex. Fine*	*Amount Minted*
1796 without stars	$8,000.00	$15,000.00	963
1796 with stars	7,200.00	10,800.00	432
1797	3,500.00	6,400.00	1,756
1798	4,800.00	6,600.00	614
1802 with 2 over 1	2,400.00	4,300.00	2,612
1804	2,400.00	4,300.00	3,327
1805	2,400.00	4,300.00	1,781
1806 with 6 over 4	2,400.00	4,300.00	1,616
1806 with 6 over 5	3,500.00	5,800.00	
1807	2,400.00	4,300.00	6,812

See page 26 regarding prices listed for gold coins.

CONDITION: *Fine:* Liberty outlined with most details visible; word LIBERTY on headband and motto on reverse worn but readable; other lettering and date sharp. *Ex. Fine:* All details of design, lettering and date sharp.

MINT MARK: None.

Date	*Fine*	*Ex. Fine*	*Amount Minted*
1808	$6,000.00	$12,000.00	2,710

1821	2,400.00	4,300.00	6,448
1824 with 4 over 1	2,400.00	4,700.00	2,600
1825	2,400.00	4,300.00	4,434
1826 with 6 over 5	3,400.00	5,400.00	760
1827	2,400.00	4,300.00	2,800
1829	2,200.00	3,600.00	3,403
1830	2,200.00	3,600.00	4,540
1831	2,200.00	3,600.00	4,520
1832	2,200.00	3,600.00	4,400
1833	2,200.00	3,600.00	4,160
1834	4,300.00	7,800.00	4,000

LIBERTY WITH RIBBON

CONDITION: *Fine:* Liberty outlined with most details visible; word LIBERTY on headband partly worn but readable; other lettering and date sharp. *Ex. Fine:* All details of design, lettering and date sharp.

MINT MARK: On obverse, above the date.

Date	*Fine*	*Ex. Fine*	*Amount Minted*
1834	$140.00	$210.00	112,234
1835	140.00	210.00	131,402
1836	140.00	210.00	547,986
1837	140.00	210.00	45,080
1838	140.00	210.00	47,030
1838-C	450.00	1,000.00	7,908
1839	140.00	210.00	27,021
1839-C	450.00	750.00	18,173
1839-D	450.00	750.00	13,674
1839-O	205.00	350.00	17,781

See page 26 regarding prices listed for gold coins.

LIBERTY WITH CORONET

CONDITION: *Fine:* Liberty outlined with most details visible; lettering and date sharp. *Ex. Fine:* All details of design, lettering and date sharp; coin should show only slight signs of wear.

MINT MARK: On reverse, below the eagle.

Date	*Fine*	*Ex. Fine*	*Amount Minted*
1840	$130.00	$170.00	18,859
1840-C	160.00	355.00	12,838
1840-D	230.00	355.00	3,532
1840-O	130.00	170.00	26,200
1841-C	185.00	355.00	10,297
1841-D	215.00	430.00	4,164
1842	195.00	390.00	2,823
1842-C	215.00	355.00	6,737
1842-D	215.00	430.00	4,643
1842-O	145.00	195.00	19,800
1843	130.00	170.00	100,546
1843-C	180.00	355.00	26,096
1843-D	180.00	355.00	36,209
1843-O	130.00	170.00	368,002
1844	165.00	225.00	6,784
1844-C	180.00	355.00	11,622
1844-D	180.00	325.00	17,332
1845	130.00	170.00	91,051
1845-D	180.00	325.00	19,460
1845-O	195.00	325.00	4,000
1846	130.00	170.00	21,598
1846-C	285.00	500.00	4,808

See page 26 regarding prices listed for gold coins.

1846-D	185.00	270.00	19,303
1846-O	130.00	170.00	66,000
1847	130.00	170.00	29,814
1847-C	185.00	270.00	23,226
1847-D	220.00	315.00	15,784
1847-O	130.00	170.00	124,000
1848	325.00	700.00	8,886
1848 with CAL.	4,000.00	7,500.00	1,389
1848-C	185.00	270.00	16,788
1848-D	215.00	270.00	13,771
1849	130.00	170.00	23,294
1849-C	220.00	315.00	10,220
1849-D	245.00	340.00	10,945
1850	130.00	170.00	252,923
1850-C	185.00	335.00	9,148
1850-D	220.00	335.00	12,148
1850-O	130.00	170.00	84,000
1851	130.00	170.00	1,372,748
1851-C	185.00	315.00	14,923
1851-D	185.00	315.00	11,264
1851-O	130.00	170.00	148,000
1852	130.00	170.00	1,159,681
1852-C	220.00	340.00	9,772
1852-D	270.00	425.00	4,078
1852-O	130.00	170.00	140,000
1853	130.00	170.00	1,404,668
1853-D	460.00	685.00	3,178
1854	130.00	170.00	596,258
1854-C	185.00	335.00	7,295
1854-D	1,050.00	1,700.00	1,760
1854-O	130.00	170.00	153,000
1854-S	5,000.00	10,000.00	246
1855	130.00	170.00	235,480
1855-C	340.00	385.00	3,677
1855-D	1,050.00	1,500.00	1,123
1856	130.00	170.00	348,240
1856-C	220.00	335.00	7,913
1856-D	1,550.00	2,600.00	874
1856-O	130.00	170.00	21,100
1856-S	130.00	170.00	71,120

See page 26 regarding prices listed for gold coins.

1857	130.00	170.00	214,130
1857-D	350.00	500.00	2,364
1857-O	130.00	170.00	34,000
1857-S	130.00	170.00	68,000
1858	130.00	170.00	47,377
1858-C	225.00	350.00	9,056
1959	130.00	170.00	39,444
1859-D	425.00	625.00	2,244
1859-S	130.00	170.00	15,200
1860	130.00	170.00	22,675
1860-C	225.00	450.00	7,469
1860-S	130.00	170.00	35,600
1861	130.00	170.00	1,272,518
1861-S	130.00	170.00	24,000
1862	130.00	170.00	112,353
1862-S	130.00	170.00	8,000
1863-S	130.00	170.00	10,800
1864	390.00	650.00	2,874
1865	390.00	715.00	1,545
1865-S	130.00	170.00	23,376
1866	190.00	455.00	3,110
1866-S	130.00	170.00	38,960
1867	170.00	390.00	3,250
1867-S	130.00	170.00	28,000
1868	165.00	325.00	3,625
1868-S	130.00	170.00	34,000
1869	165.00	260.00	4,345
1869-S	130.00	170.00	29,500
1870	155.00	225.00	4,555
1870-S	130.00	170.00	16,000
1871	155.00	195.00	5,350
1871-S	130.00	170.00	22,000
1872	165.00	215.00	3,030
1872-S	130.00	170.00	18,000
1873	130.00	170.00	178,025
1873-S	130.00	170.00	27,000
1874	155.00	195.00	3,940
1875	1,550.00	2,600.00	420
1875-S	145.00	195.00	1,160

See page 26 regarding prices listed for gold coins.

1876	130.00	170.00	4,221
1876-S	130.00	170.00	5,000
1877	200.00	500.00	1,652
1877-S	130.00	170.00	35,400
1878	130.00	170.00	286,260
1878-S	130.00	170.00	178,000
1879	130.00	170.00	88,900
1879-S	130.00	170.00	43,500
1880	220.00	350.00	2,996
1881	645.00	1,150.00	680
1882	180.00	300.00	4,040
1883	190.00	360.00	1,960
1884	190.00	360.00	1,993
1885	540.00	900.00	877
1886	155.00	210.00	4,088
1887	155.00	210.00	6,282
1888	140.00	180.00	16,098
1889	140.00	180.00	17,648
1890	140.00	180.00	8,813
1891	140.00	180.00	11,040
1892	195.00	280.00	2,545
1893	140.00	180.00	30,106
1894	170.00	210.00	4,122
1895	170.00	210.00	6,119
1896	140.00	180.00	19,202
1897	140.00	180.00	29,904
1898	140.00	180.00	24,165
1899	140.00	180.00	27,350
1900	140.00	180.00	67,205
1901	140.00	180.00	91,323
1902	140.00	180.00	133,733
1903	140.00	180.00	201,257
1904	140.00	180.00	160,960
1905	140.00	180.00	217,944
1906	140.00	180.00	176,490
1907	140.00	180.00	336,448

See page 26 regarding prices listed for gold coins.

INDIAN HEAD

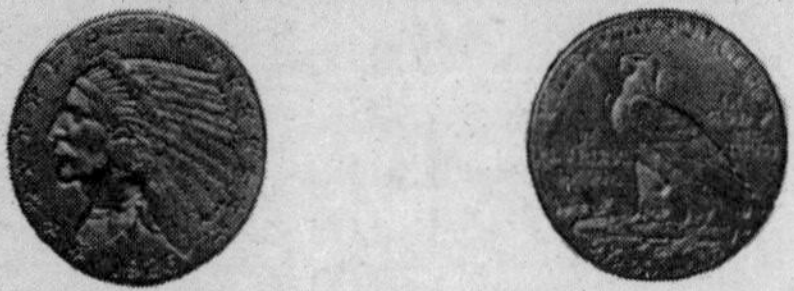

CONDITION: *Fine:* Most details of design visible; all lettering and date clear. *Ex. Fine:* All details, lettering and date sharp; coin should show only slight signs of wear.

MINT MARK: On reverse, to left of value.

Date	*Fine*	*Ex. Fine*	*Amount Minted*
1908	$130.00	$170.00	565,057
1909	130.00	170.00	441,899
1910	130.00	170.00	492,682
1911	130.00	170.00	704,191
1911-D	415.00	615.00	55,680
1912	130.00	170.00	616,197
1913	130.00	170.00	722,165
1914	130.00	170.00	240,117
1914-D	130.00	170.00	448,000
1915	130.00	170.00	606,100
1925-D	130.00	170.00	578,000
1926	130.00	170.00	446,000
1927	130.00	170.00	388,000
1928	130.00	170.00	416,000
1929	130.00	170.00	532,000

See page 26 regarding prices listed for gold coins.

21

THREE-DOLLAR GOLD PIECES

CONDITION: *Fine:* Most details of design visible; all lettering and date sharp. *Ex. Fine:* All details, lettering and date sharp.

MINT MARK: On reverse, below the wreath.

Three-dollar gold pieces were struck from 1854 to 1889. Like the silver three-cent piece, this coin was intended to facilitate the purchase of the three-cent postage stamp. This coin was never popular and in 1889, when the postage rate was changed, the three-dollar gold piece was discontinued.

Only one type of three-dollar gold piece was issued: the obverse shows Liberty wearing a feather headdress, a design similar to the one used on the 1856–89 gold dollar; the reverse shows the value and date encircled by a wreath.

Date	Fine	Ex. Fine	Amount Minted
1854	$ 550.00	$ 700.00	138,618
1854-D	3,500.00	7,500.00	1,120
1854-O	550.00	700.00	24,000
1855	550.00	700.00	50,555
1855-S	550.00	800.00	6,600
1856	550.00	700.00	26,010
1856-S	550.00	700.00	34,500
1857	550.00	700.00	20,891
1857-S	550.00	700.00	14,000
1858	590.00	1,000.00	2,133
1859	550.00	700.00	15,638
1860	550.00	700.00	7,155
1860-S	550.00	750.00	7.000
1861	550.00	750.00	6,072
1862	550.00	750.00	5,785
1863	550.00	750.00	5,039
1864	550.00	800.00	2,680
1865	720.00	1,300.00	1,165
1866	550.00	750.00	4,030
1867	550.00	750.00	2,650
1868	550.00	750.00	4,875
1869	550.00	800.00	2,525
1870	550.00	780.00	3,535
1871	640.00	850.00	1,330
1872	550.00	700.00	2,030
1874	550.00	700.00	41,820
1877	1,100.00	1,500.00	1,488
1878	550.00	700.00	82,324
1879	550.00	850.00	3,030
1880	840.00	1,100.00	1,036
1881	1,100.00	1,900.00	550
1882	770.00	950.00	1,540
1883	880.00	1,200.00	940
1884	880.00	1,300.00	1,106
1885	880.00	1,300.00	910
1886	860.00	1,150.00	1,142

See page 26 regarding prices listed for gold coins.

1887	900.00	1,350.00	6,160
1888	900.00	1,350.00	5,291
1889	900.00	1,425.00	2,429

	Proof	
1873	$ 6,000.00	25
1875	75,000.00	20
1876	20,000.00	45

See page 26 regarding prices listed for gold coins.

22

FOUR-DOLLAR GOLD PIECES (Stellas)

Four-dollar gold pieces were struck in 1879 and 1880. They were experimental coins never intended for general circulation.

Two types of obverses were used for this pattern coin, during both years of issue: one type shows Liberty with flowing hair, designed by Charles E. Barber. The second type shows Liberty with her hair coiled (not shown here), designed by George T. Morgan. The same reverse is used on both coins: a large star containing the word STELLA (Latin for *star*) and other lettering.

Four-dollar pieces of these types were struck in proof in various materials, among them aluminum and copper. Only those coins struck in gold are listed here.

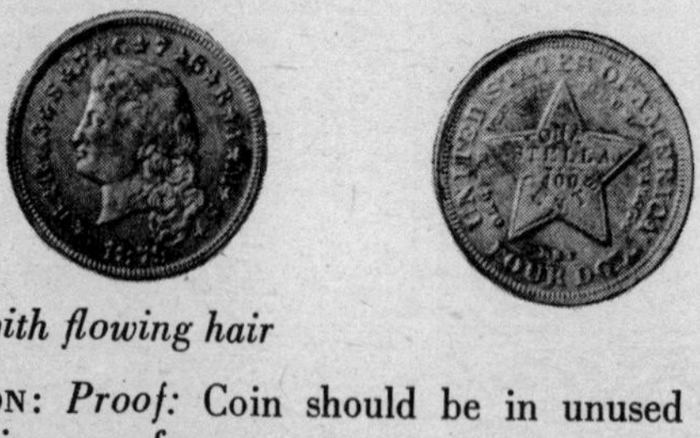

with flowing hair

CONDITION: *Proof:* Coin should be in unused condition with a mirror surface.

MINT MARK: None.

Date	*Proof*	*Amount Minted*
1879 with flowing hair	$22,500.00	415
1879 with coiled hair	75,000.00	10
1880 with flowing hair	37,500.00	15
1880 with coiled hair	75,000.00	10

23

HALF EAGLES ($5.00)

Half eagles were struck from 1795 to 1929. The value did not appear on the coin until 1807, when "5 D." was added to the reverse. In 1839, the words FIVE D. were added to designate the value. With the introduction of the Indian Head type, in 1908, the value, FIVE DOLLARS, was spelled out in full.

Five basic types of half eagles were issued: Liberty Head (1795–1807); Liberty with Draped Bust (1807–12); Liberty with Turban (1813–34); Liberty with Ribbon (1834–38); Liberty with Coronet (1839–1908); Indian Head (1908–29).

The Indian Head half eagle, designed by Bela Lyon Pratt, was struck with an incuse design (see page 164).

LIBERTY HEAD

with small eagle *with large eagle*

CONDITION: *Fine:* Liberty outlined but most details of hair worn; other details, lettering and date clear. *Ex. Fine:* All details, lettering and date sharp.

MINT MARK: None.

Date	*Fine*	*Ex. Fine*	*Amount Minted*
1795 with small eagle	$ 4,700.00	$ 7,800.00	8,707
1795 with large eagle	6,900.00	10,250.00	
1796 with small eagle	4,700.00	7,800.00	3,395
1797 with small eagle	6,200.00	10,750.00	6,406
1797 with large eagle	6,200.00	10,750.00	
1798 with small eagle	15,500.00	20,500.00	24,867
1798 with large eagle	1,900.00	2,900.00	
1799	1,900.00	2,600.00	7,451
1800	1,900.00	2,600.00	11,622
1802 with 2 over 1	1,900.00	2,600.00	53,176
1803 with 3 over 2	1,900.00	2,600.00	33,506
1804	1,900.00	2,600.00	30,475
1805	1,900.00	2,600.00	33,183
1806	1,900.00	2,600.00	64,093
1807	1,900.00	2,600.00	33,496

See page 26 regarding prices listed for gold coins.

LIBERTY WITH DRAPED BUST

CONDITION: *Fine:* Liberty outlined but most details of hair worn; word LIBERTY on headband worn but readable; other lettering and date sharp. *Ex. Fine:* All details of design, lettering and date sharp.

MINT MARK: None.

Date	*Fine*	*Ex. Fine*	*Amount Minted*
1807	$ 1,400.00	$ 2,350.00	50,597
1808	1,400.00	2,350.00	55,578
1809	1,400.00	2,350.00	33,875
1810	1,400.00	2,350.00	100,287
1811	1,400.00	2,350.00	99,581
1812	1,400.00	2,350.00	58,087

LIBERTY WITH TURBAN

CONDITION: *Fine:* Liberty outlined but some details of hair worn; word LIBERTY on headband worn but readable; other lettering and date sharp. *Ex. Fine:* All details of design, lettering and date sharp.

MINT MARK: None.

Date	*Fine*	*Ex. Fine*	*Amount Minted*
1813	$ 1,800.00	$ 2,400.00	95,428
1814	1,900.00	2,400.00	15,454
1815	11,750.00	15,500.00	635
1818	1,900.00	2,400.00	48,588
1819	9,500.00	12,500.00	51,723
1820	3,000.00	4,000.00	263,806
1821	4,000.00	8,500.00	34,641

See page 26 regarding prices listed for gold coins.

1822	75,000.00	150,000.00	17,796
1823	2,300.00	4,700.00	14,485
1824	4,000.00	9,000.00	17,340
1825	3,000.00	5,250.00	29,060
1826	3,500.00	6,000.00	18,069
1827	5,000.00	11,500.00	24,913
1828	3,500.00	9,500.00	28,029
1829	16,500.00	23,500.00	57,442
1830	3,000.00	6,250.00	126,351
1831	3,000.00	6,250.00	140,594
1832	5,500.00	8,500.00	157,487
1833	3,000.00	6,250.00	193,630
1834	3,000.00	6,250.00	50,141

LIBERTY WITH RIBBON

CONDITION: *Fine:* Liberty outlined but most details of hair worn; word LIBERTY on headband worn but readable; other lettering and date sharp. *Ex. Fine:* All details of design, lettering and date sharp; coin should show only slight signs of wear.

MINT MARK: On obverse, above the date.

Date	*Fine*	*Ex. Fine*	*Amount Minted*
1834	$ 200.00	$ 400.00	682,028
1835	200.00	400.00	371,534
1836	200.00	400.00	553,147
1837	200.00	400.00	207,121
1838	200.00	400.00	286,588
1838-C	750.00	1,600.00	12,913
1838-D	700.00	1,500.00	20,583

See page 26 regarding prices listed for gold coins.

LIBERTY WITH CORONET

without motto

CONDITION: *Fine:* Liberty outlined but most details worn; word LIBERTY on crown worn but readable; other lettering and date sharp. *Ex. Fine:* All details of design, lettering and date sharp; coin should show only slight signs of wear.

MINT MARK: On reverse, above the value.

Date	*Fine*	*Ex. Fine*	*Amount Minted*
1839	$ 150.00	$ 200.00	118,143
1839-C	310.00	925.00	23,467
1839-D	310.00	925.00	18,939
1840	150.00	200.00	137,382
1840-C	310.00	540.00	19,028
1840-D	285.00	485.00	22,896
1840-O	170.00	210.00	30,400
1841	150.00	200.00	15,833
1841-C	230.00	440.00	21,511
1841-D	215.00	400.00	30,495
1842	150.00	200.00	27,578
1842-C	310.00	420.00	27,480
1842-D	285.00	385.00	59,608
1842-O	175.00	265.00	16,400
1843	150.00	200.00	611,205
1843-C	255.00	370.00	44,353
1843-D	230.00	330.00	98,452
1843-O	155.00	210.00	101,075
1844	150.00	200.00	340,330

See page 26 regarding prices listed for gold coins.

1844-C	275.00	460.00	23,631
1844-D	255.00	425.00	88,982
1844-O	160.00	190.00	364,600
1845	150.00	200.00	417,099
1845-D	255.00	365.00	90,629
1845-O	160.00	200.00	41,000
1846	150.00	200.00	395,942
1846-C	340.00	595.00	12,995
1846-D	315.00	460.00	80,294
1846-O	155.00	200.00	58,000
1847	150.00	200.00	915,981
1847-C	340.00	500.00	84,151
1847-D	315.00	460.00	64,405
1847-O	175.00	225.00	12,000
1848	150.00	200.00	260,775
1848-C	340.00	500.00	64,472
1848-D	315.00	460.00	47,465
1849	150.00	200.00	133,070
1849-C	275.00	425.00	64,823
1849-D	255.00	385.00	39,036
1850	150.00	200.00	64,491
1850-C	275.00	425.00	63,591
1850-D	255.00	385.00	43,950
1851	150.00	200.00	377,505
1851-C	340.00	425.00	49,176
1851-D	315.00	385.00	62,710
1851-O	160.00	225.00	41,000
1852	150.00	200.00	573,901
1852-C	275.00	460.00	72,574
1852-D	255.00	425.00	91,452
1853	150.00	200.00	305,770
1853-C	275.00	460.00	65,571
1853-D	255.00	425.00	89,678
1854	150.00	200.00	160,675
1854-C	275.00	500.00	39,291
1854-D	255.00	385.00	56,413
1854-O	160.00	225.00	46,000
1854-S	10,500.00	21,000.00	268
1855	150.00	200.00	117,098

See page 26 regarding prices listed for gold coins.

1855-C	330.00	460.00	39,788
1855-D	300.00	425.00	22,432
1855-O	150.00	230.00	11,100
1855-S	150.00	200.00	61,000
1856	150.00	200.00	197,990
1856-C	330.00	425.00	28,457
1856-D	300.00	425.00	19,786
1856-O	150.00	200.00	10,000
1856-S	150.00	200.00	105,100
1857	150.00	200.00	98,188
1857-C	270.00	425.00	31,360
1857-D	250.00	400.00	17,046
1857-O	150.00	200.00	13,000
1857-S	150.00	200.00	87,000
1858	150.00	210.00	15,136
1858-C	330.00	385.00	38,856
1858-D	300.00	400.00	15,362
1858-S	150.00	200.00	18,600
1859	150.00	200.00	16,814
1859-C	330.00	385.00	31,847
1859-D	300.00	365.00	10,366
1859-S	150.00	200.00	13,220
1860	150.00	200.00	19,825
1860-C	270.00	425.00	14,813
1860-D	250.00	400.00	14,635
1860-S	150.00	200.00	21,200
1861	150.00	200.00	639,950
1861-C	575.00	1,000.00	6,879
1861-D	1,225.00	3,000.00	1,597
1861-S	150.00	200.00	18,000
1862	170.00	380.00	4,465
1862-S	150.00	230.00	9,500
1863	370.00	700.00	2,472
1863-S	185.00	265.00	17,000
1864	310.00	540.00	4,220
1864-S	370.00	735.00	3,888
1865	540.00	925.00	1,295
1865-S	185.00	230.00	27,612
1866-S**	210.00	310.00	43,920

See page 26 regarding prices listed for gold coins.

with motto

Date	*Fine*	*Ex. Fine*	*Amount Minted*
1866	$250.00	$460.00	6,720
1866-S**	205.00	285.00	part of above
1867	250.00	500.00	6,920
1867-S	190.00	275.00	29,000
1868	250.00	420.00	5,725
1868-S	190.00	230.00	52,000
1869	420.00	890.00	1,785
1869-S	190.00	250.00	31,000
1870	250.00	330.00	4,035
1870-CC	500.00	1,000.00	7,675
1870-S	195.00	230.00	17,000
1871	250.00	435.00	3,230
1871-CC	205.00	400.00	20,770
1871-S	195.00	230.00	25,000
1872	420.00	890.00	1,690
1872-CC	215.00	400.00	16,980
1872-S	190.00	230.00	36,400
1873	150.00	200.00	112,505
1873-CC	250.00	450.00	7,416
1873-S	170.00	230.00	31,000
1874	215.00	420.00	3,508
1874-CC	215.00	350.00	21,198
1874-S	190.00	230.00	16,000
1875	2,300.00	7,350.00	220
1875-CC	215.00	350.00	11,828
1875-S	205.00	230.00	9,000
1876	420.00	680.00	1,477

See page 26 regarding prices listed for gold coins.

1876-CC	225.00	500.00	6,887
1876-S	180.00	370.00	4,000
1877	370.00	735.00	1,152
1877-CC	225.00	500.00	8,680
1877-S	150.00	200.00	26,700
1878	150.00	200.00	131,740
1878-CC	500.00	1,250.00	9,054
1878-S	150.00	170.00	144,700
1879	150.00	170.00	301,950
1879-CC	175.00	250.00	17,281
1879-S	150.00	170.00	426,200
1880	150.00	170.00	3,166,436
1880-CC	150.00	190.00	51,017
1880-S	150.00	170.00	1,348,900
1881	150.00	170.00	5,708,800
1881-CC	175.00	240.00	13,886
1881-S	150.00	170.00	969,000
1882	150.00	170.00	2,514,560
1882-CC	150.00	170.00	82,817
1882-S	150.00	170.00	969,999
1883	150.00	170.00	233,440
1883-CC	150.00	190.00	12,958
1883-S	150.00	170.00	83,200
1884	150.00	170.00	191,048
1884-CC	150.00	190.00	16,402
1884-D	150.00	170.00	177,000
1885	150.00	170.00	601,506
1885-S	150.00	170.00	1,211,500
1886	150.00	170.00	388,432
1886-S	150.00	170.00	3,268,000
1887-S	150.00	170.00	1,912,000
1888	150.00	170.00	18,296
1888-S	150.00	170.00	293,900
1889	150.00	270.00	7,565
1890	150.00	290.00	4,328
1890-CC	150.00	170.00	53,800
1891	150.00	170.00	61,413
1891-CC	150.00	170.00	208,000
1892	150.00	170.00	753,572

See page 26 regarding prices listed for gold coins.

1892-CC	150.00	190.00	82,968
1892-O	350.00	600.00	10,000
1892-S	150.00	170.00	298,400
1893	150.00	170.00	1,528,197
1893-CC	150.00	190.00	60,000
1893-O	150.00	190.00	110,000
1893-S	150.00	170.00	224,000
1894	150.00	170.00	957,955
1894-O	150.00	190.00	16,600
1894-S	150.00	170.00	55,900
1895	150.00	170.00	1,345,936
1895-S	150.00	170.00	112,000
1896	150.00	170.00	59,063
1896-S	150.00	170.00	155,400
1897	150.00	170.00	867,883
1897-S	150.00	170.00	354,000
1898	150.00	170.00	633,495
1898-S	150.00	170.00	1,397,400
1899	150.00	170.00	1,710,729
1899-S	150.00	170.00	1,545,000
1900	150.00	170.00	1,405,730
1900-S	150.00	170.00	329,000
1901	150.00	170.00	616,040
1901-S	150.00	170.00	3,648,000
1902	150.00	170.00	172,562
1902-S	150.00	170.00	939,000
1903	150.00	170.00	227,024
1903-S	150.00	170.00	1,855,000
1904	150.00	170.00	392,136
1904-S	150.00	170.00	97,000
1905	150.00	170.00	302,308
1905-S	150.00	170.00	880,700
1906	150.00	170.00	348,820
1906-D	150.00	170.00	320,000
1906-S	150.00	170.00	598,000
1907	150.00	170.00	626,192
1907-D	150.00	170.00	888,000
1908	150.00	170.00	421,874

See page 26 regarding prices listed for gold coins.

INDIAN HEAD

CONDITION: *Fine:* Most details of design visible; lettering and date clear. *Ex. Fine:* All details of design, lettering and date sharp; coin should show only slight signs of wear.

MINT MARK: On reverse, to left of value.

Date	*Fine*	*Ex. Fine*	*Amount Minted*
1908	$160.00	$200.00	578,012
1908-D	160.00	200.00	148,000
1908-S	190.00	250.00	82,000
1909	160.00	200.00	627,138
1909-D	160.00	200.00	3,423,560
1909-O	225.00	400.00	34,200
1909-S	160.00	200.00	297,200
1910	160.00	200.00	604,250
1910-D	160.00	200.00	193,600
1910-S	160.00	200.00	770,200
1911	160.00	200.00	915,139
1911-D	160.00	200.00	72,500
1911-S	160.00	200.00	1,416,000
1912	160.00	200.00	790,144
1912-S	160.00	200.00	392,000
1913	160.00	200.00	916,099
1913-S	160.00	200.00	408,000
1914	160.00	200.00	247,125
1914-D	160.00	200.00	247,000
1914-S	160.00	200.00	263,000
1915	160.00	200.00	588,075
1915-S	160.00	200.00	164,000
1916-S	160.00	200.00	240,000
1929	2,000.00	3,500.00	662,000

See page 26 regarding prices listed for gold coins.

24

EAGLES ($10.00)

Eagles were struck from 1795 to 1933. The value did not appear on the coin until 1838, when the words TEN D. were added to the reverse. In 1907, with the Indian Head type, the value, TEN DOLLARS, was spelled out in full.

The following types of eagles were issued: Liberty Head (1795–1804); Liberty with Coronet (1838–1907); Indian Head (1907–33).

The Indian Head type, which actually shows Liberty wearing an Indian war bonnet, was designed by Augustus Saint-Gaudens. On the edge of the 1907–11 coins are 46 raised stars, representing the states of the Union. In 1912, with the admission of New Mexico and Arizona to the Union, two more stars were added to the coin edge.

LIBERTY HEAD

with small eagle

with large eagle

CONDITION: *Fine:* Liberty outlined but most details worn; lettering and date sharp. *Ex. Fine:* All details of design, lettering and date sharp.

MINT MARK: None.

Date	*Fine*	*Ex. Fine*	*Amount Minted*
1795 with small eagle	$ 5,800.00	$ 9,000.00	2,795
1796 with small eagle	5,800.00	8,400.00	6,080
1797 with small eagle	5,800.00	8,400.00	9,177
1797 with large eagle	2,800.00	4,300.00	
1798 with 8 over 7; with 4 stars	4,700.00	9,000.00	7,974
1798 with 8 over 7; with 6 stars	10,800.00	24,000.00	
1799	2,400.00	4,000.00	17,483
1800	2,400.00	4,000.00	25,965
1801	2,400.00	4,000.00	29,254
1803	2,400.00	4,000.00	8,979
1804	3,600.00	4,800.00	9,795

See page 26 regarding prices listed for gold coins.

LIBERTY WITH CORONET

without motto

CONDITION: *Fine:* Liberty outlined but most hair details worn; word LIBERTY on crown worn but readable; other lettering and date sharp. *Ex. Fine:* All details of design, lettering and date sharp; coin should show only slight signs of wear.

MINT MARK: On reverse, below the eagle.

Date	*Fine*	*Ex. Fine*	*Amount Minted*
1838	$ 500.00	$1,200.00	7,200
1839	500.00	1,200.00	38,248
1840	250.00	300.00	47,338
1841	250.00	300.00	63,131
1841-O	350.00	650.00	2,500
1842	250.00	300.00	81,507
1842-O	250.00	300.00	27,400
1843	250.00	300.00	75,462
1843-O	250.00	300.00	175,162
1844	300.00	350.00	6,361
1844-O	250.00	300.00	118,700
1845	250.00	300.00	26,153
1845-O	250.00	300.00	47,500
1846	250.00	300.00	20,095
1846-O	250.00	300.00	81,780
1847	250.00	300.00	862,258
1847-O	250.00	300.00	571,500

See page 26 regarding prices listed for gold coins.

1848	250.00	300.00	145,484
1848-O	250.00	300.00	35,850
1849	250.00	300.00	653,618
1849-O	250.00	300.00	23,900
1850	250.00	300.00	291,451
1850-O	250.00	300.00	57,500
1851	250.00	300.00	176,328
1851-O	250.00	300.00	263,000
1852	250.00	300.00	263,106
1852-O	300.00	400.00	18,000
1853	250.00	300.00	201,253
1853-O	250.00	300.00	51,000
1854	250.00	300.00	54,250
1854-O	300.00	400.00	52,500
1854-S	250.00	300.00	123,826
1855	250.00	300.00	121,701
1855-O	350.00	450.00	18,000
1855-S	400.00	600.00	9,000
1856	250.00	300.00	60,490
1856-O	250.00	300.00	14,500
1856-S	250.00	300.00	68,000
1857	275.00	350.00	16,606
1857-O	350.00	475.00	5,500
1857-S	250.00	300.00	26,000
1858	2,500.00	3,500.00	2,521
1858-O	250.00	300.00	20,000
1858-S	250.00	300.00	11,800
1859	250.00	300.00	16,093
1859-O	350.00	625.00	2,300
1859-S	250.00	300.00	7,000
1860	250.00	300.00	11,783
1860-O	250.00	300.00	11,100
1860-S	250.00	400.00	5,000
1861	250.00	300.00	113,233
1861-S	250.00	300.00	15,500
1862	275.00	385.00	10,995
1862-S	275.00	375.00	12,500
1863	650.00	1,150.00	1,248
1863-S	285.00	550.00	10,000

See page 26 regarding prices listed for gold coins.

1864	385.00	700.00	3,580
1864-S	550.00	975.00	2,500
1865	350.00	700.00	4,005
1865-S	325.00	400.00	16,700
1866-S	325.00	550.00	20,000

with motto

Date	*Fine*	*Ex. Fine*	*Amount Minted*
1866	$ 375.00	$ 615.00	3,780
1866-S	275.00	425.00	included above
1867	385.00	615.00	3,140
1867-S	275.00	385.00	9,000
1868	275.00	375.00	10,655
1868-S	275.00	300.00	13,500
1869	550.00	850.00	1,855
1869-S	285.00	300.00	6,430
1870	300.00	575.00	2,535
1870-CC	500.00	1,250.00	5,908
1870-S	285.00	375.00	8,000
1871	550.00	850.00	1,780
1871-CC	350.00	500.00	7,185
1871-S	275.00	300.00	16,500
1872	550.00	775.00	1,650
1872-CC	350.00	550.00	5,500
1872-S	275.00	300.00	17,300
1873	1,300.00	2,250.00	825
1873-CC	350.00	500.00	4,543
1873-S	275.00	300.00	12,000

See page 26 regarding prices listed for gold coins.

1874	250.00	300.00	53,160
1874-CC	300.00	350.00	16,767
1874-S	250.00	300.00	10,000
1875	7,700.00	15,500.00	120
1875-CC	300.00	550.00	7,715
1876	1,250.00	2,100.00	732
1876-CC	300.00	550.00	4,696
1876-S	290.00	300.00	5,000
1877	1,250.00	1,550.00	817
1877-CC	400.00	625.00	3,332
1877-S	250.00	300.00	17,000
1878	250.00	300.00	73,800
1878-CC	550.00	1,000.00	3,244
1878-S	250.00	300.00	26,100
1879	250.00	275.00	384,770
1879-CC	500.00	1,500.00	1,762
1879-O	500.00	1,500.00	1,500
1879-S	250.00	275.00	224,000
1880	250.00	275.00	1,644,876
1880-CC	300.00	350.00	11,190
1880-O	325.00	400.00	9,200
1880-S	250.00	275.00	506,250
1881	250.00	275.00	3,877,260
1881-CC	300.00	350.00	24,015
1881-O	350.00	450.00	8,350
1881-S	250.00	275.00	970,000
1882	250.00	275.00	2,324,480
1882-CC	300.00	400.00	6,764
1882-O	250.00	275.00	10,820
1882-S	250.00	275.00	132,000
1883	250.00	275.00	208,740
1883-CC	300.00	350.00	12,000
1883-O	800.00	1,250.00	800
1883-S	250.00	275.00	38,000
1884	250.00	275.00	76,905
1884-CC	300.00	350.00	9,925
1884-S	250.00	275.00	124,250
1885	250.00	275.00	253,527
1885-S	250.00	275.00	228,000
1886	250.00	275.00	236,160

See page 26 regarding prices listed for gold coins.

1886-S	250.00	275.00	826,000
1887	250.00	275.00	53,680
1887-S	250.00	275.00	817,000
1888	250.00	275.00	132,996
1888-O	250.00	275.00	21,335
1888-S	250.00	275.00	648,700
1889	300.00	350.00	4,485
1889-S	250.00	275.00	425,400
1890	250.00	275.00	58,043
1890-CC	250.00	275.00	17,500
1891	250.00	275.00	91,868
1891-CC	250.00	275.00	103,732
1892	250.00	275.00	797,552
1892-CC	250.00	275.00	40,000
1892-O	250.00	275.00	28,688
1892-S	250.00	275.00	115,500
1893	250.00	275.00	1,840,895
1893-CC	300.00	350.00	14,000
1893-O	250.00	275.00	17,000
1893-S	250.00	275.00	141,350
1894	250.00	275.00	2,470,778
1894-O	250.00	275.00	107,500
1894-S	275.00	300.00	25,000
1895	250.00	275.00	567,826
1895-O	250.00	275.00	98,000
1895-S	250.00	275.00	49,000
1896	250.00	275.00	76,348
1896-S	250.00	275.00	123,750
1897	250.00	275.00	1,000,159
1897-O	250.00	275.00	42,500
1897-S	250.00	275.00	234,750
1898	250.00	275.00	812,197
1898-S	250.00	275.00	473,600
1899	250.00	275.00	1,262,305
1899-O	250.00	275.00	37,047
1899-S	250.00	275.00	841,000
1900	250.00	275.00	293,960
1900-S	250.00	275.00	81,000
1901	250.00	275.00	1,718,825
1901-O	250.00	275.00	72.041

See page 26 regarding prices listed for gold coins.

1901-S	250.00	275.00	2,812,750
1902	250.00	275.00	82,513
1902-S	250.00	275.00	469,500
1903	250.00	275.00	125,926
1903-O	250.00	275.00	112,771
1903-S	250.00	275.00	538,000
1904	250.00	275.00	162,038
1904-O	250.00	275.00	108,950
1905	250.00	275.00	201,078
1905-S	250.00	275.00	369,250
1906	250.00	275.00	165,497
1906-D	250.00	275.00	981,000
1906-O	250.00	275.00	86,895
1906-S	250.00	275.00	457,000
1907	250.00	275.00	1,203,973
1907-D	250.00	275.00	1,030,000
1907-S	250.00	275.00	210,500

See page 26 regarding prices listed for gold coins.

INDIAN HEAD

with periods

without periods

CONDITION: *Fine:* Indian head outlined with most details visible; word LIBERTY on headband worn but readable; other lettering and date sharp. *Ex. Fine:* All details of design, lettering and date sharp; coin should show only slight signs of wear.

MINT MARK: On reverse, to left of value.

Date	*Fine*	*Ex. Fine*	*Amount Minted*
1907	$ 300.00	$ 350.00	239,406
1907 with wire edge; periods at legend	2,000.00	4,000.00	500
1907 with rolled edge; periods at legend	10,000.00	15,000.00	42
1908 without motto	375.00	425.00	33,500
1908 with motto	300.00	350.00	341,486
1908-D without motto	300.00	350.00	210,000
1908-D with motto	300.00	350.00	836,500
1908-S	350.00	400.00	59,853
1909	300.00	350.00	184,860
1909-D	300.00	350.00	121,540
1909-S	300.00	350.00	292,350
1910	300.00	350.00	318,704
1910-D	300.00	350.00	2,356,640
1910-S	300.00	350.00	811,000
1911	300.00	350.00	505,595
1911-D	350.00	400.00	30,100
1911-S	300.00	350.00	51,000
1912	300.00	350.00	405,083
1912-S	300.00	350.00	300,000
1913	300.00	350.00	442,071
1913-S	350.00	400.00	66,000
1914	300.00	350.00	151,050
1914-D	300.00	350.00	343,500
1914-S	300.00	350.00	208,000
1915	300.00	350.00	351,075
1915-S	350.00	400.00	59,000
1916-S	300.00	350.00	138,500
1920-S	5,000.00	12,500.00	126,500
1926	300.00	350.00	1,014,000
1930-S	5,000.00	12,500.00	98,000
1932	300.00	350.00	4,463,000
1933	20,000.00	55,000.00	312,000

See page 26 regarding prices listed for gold coins.

25

DOUBLE EAGLES

($20.00)

Double eagles were struck from 1849 to 1933. This twenty-dollar denomination is the highest for any coin issued by the U. S. Mint for general circulation. Like the gold dollar, this coin came into existence with the discovery of gold in California.

Only two types of double eagles were issued: Liberty Head (1849–1907) and Liberty Standing (1907–33). The latter type is also known as "Saint-Gaudens" type, after its designer, Augustus Saint-Gaudens.

LIBERTY HEAD

without motto

CONDITION: *Fine:* Liberty outlined with most details visible: word LIBERTY on crown worn but readable; other lettering and date sharp. *Ex. Fine:* All details of design, lettering and date sharp; coin should show only slight signs of wear.

MINT MARK: On reverse, below the eagle.

Date	*Fine*	*Ex. Fine*	*Amount Minted*
1849 pattern coin in Mint collection	—	—	—
1850	$ 550.00	$ 600.00	1,170,261
1850-O	575.00	650.00	141,000
1851	550.00	600.00	2,087,155
1851-O	575.00	650.00	315,000
1852	550.00	600.00	2,053,026
1852-O	575.00	650.00	190,000
1853	550.00	600.00	1,261,326
1853-O	575.00	650.00	71,000
1854	550.00	600.00	757,899
1854-O	12,500.00	15,000.00	3,250
1854-S	550.00	600.00	141,468
1855	550.00	600.00	364,666
1855-O	600.00	800.00	8,000
1855-S	550.00	600.00	879,675
1856	550.00	600.00	329,878
1856-O	12,500.00	17,500.00	2,250
1856-S	550.00	600.00	1,189,750
1857	550.00	600.00	439,375
1857-O	675.00	900.00	30,000
1857-S	550.00	600.00	970,500
1858	550.00	600.00	211,714
1858-O	600.00	750.00	35,250
1858-S	550.00	600.00	846,710
1859	550.00	600.00	43,597
1859-O	1,000.00	1,650.00	9,100
1859-S	550.00	600.00	636,445
1860	550.00	600.00	577,670
1860-O	1,000.00	1,750.00	6,600

See page 26 regarding prices listed for gold coins.

1860-S	550.00	600.00	544,950
1861	550.00	600.00	2,976,453
1861-O	1,200.00	2,000.00	5,000
1861-S	550.00	600.00	768,000
1862	600.00	700.00	92,133
1862-S	550.00	600.00	854,173
1863	550.00	600.00	142,790
1863-S	550.00	600.00	966,570
1864	550.00	600.00	204,285
1864-S	550.00	600.00	793,660
1865	550.00	600.00	351,200
1865-S	550.00	600.00	1,042,500
1866-S	600.00	750.00	842,250

with motto

Date	*Fine*	*Ex. Fine*	*Amount Minted*
1866	$ 550.00	$ 575.00	698,775
1866-S	550.00	575.00	included above
1867	550.00	575.00	251,065
1867-S	550.00	575.00	920,750
1868	550.00	575.00	98,600
1868-S	550.00	575.00	837,500
1869	550.00	575.00	175,155
1869-S	550.00	575.00	686,750
1870	550.00	575.00	155,185
1870-CC	7,500.00	12,500.00	3,789

See page 26 regarding prices listed for gold coins.

1870-S	550.00	575.00	982,000
1871	550.00	575.00	80,150
1871-CC	650.00	750.00	14,687
1871-S	550.00	575.00	928,000
1872	550.00	575.00	251,880
1872-CC	650.00	775.00	29,650
1872-S	550.00	575.00	780,000
1873	550.00	575.00	1,709,825
1873-CC	650.00	750.00	22,410
1873-S	550.00	575.00	1,040,600
1874	550.00	575.00	366,800
1874-CC	575.00	600.00	115,085
1874-S	550.00	575.00	1,214,100
1875	550.00	575.00	295,740
1875-CC	575.00	600.00	1,111,151
1875-S	550.00	575.00	1,230,000
1876	550.00	575.00	583,905
1876-CC	575.00	600.00	138,441
1876-S	550.00	575.00	1,597,000
1877	550.00	575.00	397,670
1877-CC	575.00	600.00	42,565
1877-S	550.00	575.00	1,735,000
1878	550.00	575.00	543,645
1878-CC	650.00	750.00	13,180
1878-S	550.00	575.00	1,739,000
1879	550.00	575.00	207,630
1879-CC	750.00	1,000.00	10,708
1879-O	1,000.00	1,750.00	2,325
1879-S	550.00	575.00	1,223,800
1880	550.00	575.00	51,456
1880-S	550.00	575.00	836,000
1881	2,500.00	4,000.00	2,260
1881-S	550.00	575.00	727,000
1882	5,000.00	9,000.00	630
1882-CC	575.00	600.00	39,140
1882-S	550.00	575.00	1,125,000
1883-CC	575.00	600.00	59,962
1883-S	550.00	575.00	1,189,000
1884-CC	575.00	600.00	81,139
1884-S	550.00	575.00	916,000

See page 26 regarding prices listed for gold coins.

1885	2,500.00	4,500.00	828
1885-CC	650.00	750.00	9,450
1885-S	550.00	575.00	683,500
1886	3,500.00	6,500.00	1,106
1887-S	550.00	575.00	283,000
1888	550.00	575.00	226,266
1888-S	550.00	575.00	859,000
1889	550.00	575.00	44,111
1889-CC	575.00	600.00	30,945
1889-S	550.00	575.00	774,700
1890	550.00	575.00	75,995
1890-CC	575.00	600.00	91,209
1890-S	550.00	575.00	802,750
1891	1,500.00	2,500.00	1,442
1891-CC	750.00	1,500.00	5,000
1891-S	550.00	575.00	1,288,125
1892	1,500.00	2,000.00	4,523
1892-CC	600.00	750.00	27,265
1892-S	550.00	575.00	930,150
1893	550.00	575.00	344,339
1893-CC	750.00	1,000.00	18,402
1893-S	550.00	575.00	996,175
1894	550.00	575.00	1,368,990
1894-S	550.00	575.00	1,048,550
1895	550.00	575.00	1,114,656
1895-S	550.00	575.00	1,143,500
1896	550.00	575.00	792,663
1896-S	550.00	575.00	1,403,925
1897	550.00	575.00	1,383,261
1897-S	550.00	575.00	1,470,250
1898	550.00	575.00	170,470
1898-S	550.00	575.00	2,575,175
1899	550.00	575.00	1,669,384
1899-S	550.00	575.00	2,010,300
1900	550.00	575.00	1,874,584
1900-S	550.00	575.00	2,459,500
1901	550.00	575.00	111,526
1901-S	550.00	575.00	1,596,000
1902	575.00	600.00	31,254

See page 26 regarding prices listed for gold coins.

1902-S	550.00	575.00	1,753,625
1903	550.00	575.00	287,428
1903-S	550.00	575.00	954,000
1904	550.00	575.00	6,256,797
1904-S	550.00	575.00	5,134,175
1905	575.00	600.00	59,011
1905-S	550.00	575.00	1,183,000
1906	575.00	600.00	69,690
1906-D	550.00	575.00	620,250
1906-S	550.00	575.00	2,065,750
1907	550.00	575.00	1,451,864
1907-D	550.00	575.00	842,250
1907-S	550.00	575.00	2,165,800

	Proof	
1883	$45,000.00	40
1884	37,500.00	71
1887	22,500.00	121

See page 26 regarding prices listed for gold coins.

LIBERTY STANDING

dated MCMVII *with no motto*

with motto

CONDITION: *Fine:* Liberty outlined, but most details of drapery worn; all lettering and date sharp. *Ex. Fine:* All details of design, lettering and date sharp; coin should show only slight signs of wear.

MINT MARK: On obverse, above the date.

Date	*Fine*	*Unc.*	*Amount Minted*
1907 dated MCMVII	$2,250.00	$4,000.00	361,667
1907	575.00	600.00	11,250
1908 without motto	575.00	600.00	4,271,551
1908-D with motto	575.00	600.00	349,500
1908-D without motto	575.00	600.00	663,750
1908-S	650.00	750.00	22,000
1909	575.00	600.00	161,282 (1909 and 1909 with 09 over 08 combined)
1909 with 09 over 08	600.00	625.00	
1909-D	600.00	625.00	52,500
1909-S	575.00	600.00	2,774,925
1910	575.00	600.00	482,167
1910-D	575.00	600.00	429,000
1910-S	575.00	600.00	2,128,250
1911	575.00	600.00	197,350
1911-D	575.00	600.00	846,500
1911-S	575.00	600.00	775,750

See page 26 regarding prices listed for gold coins.

1912	575.00	600.00	149,824
1913	575.00	600.00	168,838
1913-D	575.00	600.00	393,500
1913-S	700.00	800.00	34,000
1914	575.00	600.00	95,320
1914-D	575.00	600.00	453,000
1914-S	575.00	600.00	1,498,000
1915	575.00	600.00	152,050
1915-S	575.00	600.00	567,500
1916-S	575.00	600.00	796,000
1920	575.00	600.00	228,250
1920-S	2,500.00	4,000.00	558,000
1921	5,000.00	7,500.00	528,500
1922	575.00	600.00	1,375,500
1922-S	700.00	850.00	2,658,000
1923	575.00	600.00	566,000
1923-D	600.00	650.00	1,702,250
1924	575.00	600.00	4,323,500
1924-D	800.00	1,200.00	3,049,500
1924-S	800.00	1,200.00	2,927,500
1925	575.00	600.00	2,831,750
1925-D	800.00	1,200.00	2,938,500
1925-S	800.00	1,200.00	3,776,500
1926	575.00	600.00	816,750
1926-D	1,000.00	2,000.00	481,000
1926-S	800.00	1,000.00	2,041,500
1927	575.00	600.00	2,946,750
1927-D	35,000.00	95,000.00	180,000
1927-S	1,500.00	2,500.00	3,107,000
1928	575.00	600.00	8,816,000
1929	3,250.00	6,500.00	1,779,750
1930-S	6,500.00	13,000.00	74,000
1931	6,500.00	13,000.00	2,938,250
1931-D	6,500.00	13,000.00	106,500
1932	6,500.00	13,000.00	1,101,750
1933 withheld from circulation			445,500

See page 26 regarding prices listed for gold coins.

26

U.S. COMMEMORATIVE COINS

Coins that commemorate an historical event, place, or person have been struck since the earliest days of coinage. U.S. Commemorative coins have the distinction of being among the most beautiful of such coins issued.

Authorized by an act of Congress, commemorative coins are struck at the Mint and generally turned over to a commission in charge of the event being commemorated. The commission usually purchases the coins at face value and sells them, usually at a price higher than face value, as souvenirs or keepsakes to help raise funds for a monument or celebration to honor the event. These coins are issued in comparatively small amounts and usually for a very limited time.

U. S. Commemorative coins have been struck in silver and gold from 1892 to 1954; no commemorative coins have been struck in this country since 1954. The coinage figures listed in this section represent those coins available at the present time; allowance has been made for commemorative coins that have been returned to the Mint and melted down.

Since commemorative coins were never intended for general circulation, they are usually in demand only in uncirculated or extremely fine condition; those coins which show signs of wear generally bring a price much lower than coins in bright, new condition.

27

SILVER COMMEMORATIVE COINS

A total of fifty different types of silver U. S. Commemorative coins has been issued. Of these, 48 are half-dollar denominations; the remaining coins are a quarter-dollar piece and a one-dollar piece.

Coins in this section are listed in chronological order.

CONDITION (for all coins in this section): *Ex. Fine:* All details of design, lettering, and date sharp; coin should show only slight signs of wear. *Unc.:* Coin should be in unused condition.

COLUMBIAN EXPOSITION

This half dollar was issued in 1892 and 1893 for the Columbian Exposition in Chicago to commemorate the 400th anniversary of the discovery of America. The obverse, designed by Charles E. Barber, shows a bust of Columbus; the reverse, designed by George T. Morgan, shows the flagship *Santa Maria* over two hemispheres.

Date	*Ex. Fine*	*Unc.*	*Amount Available*
1892	$3.50	$15.00	950,000
1893	3.50	12.50	1,548,300

ISABELLA QUARTER DOLLAR

This quarter dollar was issued in 1893 by petition of the Board of Lady Managers of the Columbian Exposition (see above). The coin was designed by Charles E. Barber. The obverse shows a bust of Isabella of Spain; the reverse shows a kneeling woman with distaff and spindle, representative of woman's industry.

Date	*Ex. Fine*	*Unc.*	*Amount Available*
1893	$110.00	$300.00	24,191

LAFAYETTE DOLLAR

This dollar was issued in 1900 for the Lafayette Memorial Commission to raise funds for a statue of Lafayette to be presented to the city of Paris as a gift from the people of America. The coin was designed by Charles E. Barber. The obverse shows the heads of Lafayette and George Washington; the reverse shows the memorial statue to be presented.

Date	*Ex. Fine*	*Unc.*	*Amount Available*
1900	$200.00	$850.00	36,026

PANAMA-PACIFIC EXPOSITION

This half dollar was issued in 1915 for the Panama-Pacific Exposition in San Francisco to celebrate the opening of the Panama Canal. The coin was designed by Charles E. Barber. The obverse shows Columbia standing with a child; in the background is a setting sun and the Golden Gate Bridge. The reverse shows an eagle with spread wings standing on a U. S. shield.

Date	*Ex. Fine*	*Unc.*	*Amount Available*
1915-S	$75.00	$600.00	27,134

ILLINOIS CENTENNIAL

This half dollar was issued in 1918 to commemorate the 100th anniversary of the admission of Illinois into the Union. The obverse, designed by George T. Morgan, shows a bust of young Abraham Lincoln; the reverse, designed by John R. Sinnock, shows an eagle standing on U. S. shield.

Date	*Ex. Fine*	*Unc.*	*Amount Available*
1918	$35.00	$85.00	100,058

MAINE CENTENNIAL

This half dollar was issued in 1920 to commemorate the 100th anniversary of the admission of Maine into the Union. The coin was designed by Anthony de Francisci. The obverse shows the arms of Maine. The reverse shows a wreath of pine needles and cones.

Date	*Ex. Fine*	*Unc.*	*Amount Available*
1920	$15.00	$115.00	50,028

PILGRIM TERCENTENARY

This half dollar was issued in 1920 and 1921 to commemorate the 300th anniversary of the landing of the Pilgrims at Plymouth, Massachusetts, in 1620. The coin was designed by Cyrus E. Dallin. The obverse shows a half figure of Governor Bradford. The reverse shows the ship *Mayflower*. The 1920 issue shows dates 1620–1920 on reverse, with no date on obverse. The following year, the date 1921 was added to the obverse.

Date	*Ex. Fine*	*Unc.*	*Amount Available*
1920	$10.00	$ 55.00	152,000
1921	20.00	115.00	20,053

MISSOURI CENTENNIAL

This half dollar was issued in 1921 to commemorate the 100th anniversary of the admission of Missouri into the Union. The coin was designed by Robert Aitken. The obverse shows a bust of an early frontiersman wearing a coonskin hat. The reverse shows a frontiersman and an Indian standing; in the field are 24 stars representing the total number of states in the Union at the time of Missouri's admission.

Date	*Ex. Fine*	*Unc.*	*Amount Available*
1921	$120.00	$890.00	15,400
1921 with 2 ★ 4 in field on obverse	135.00	925.00	5,000

ALABAMA CENTENNIAL

This half dollar was issued in 1921 to commemorate the 100th anniversary of the admission of Alabama into the Union (the 100th anniversary actually took place in 1919). The coin was designed by Laura G. Fraser. The obverse shows busts of William Wyatt Bibb, the first governor of Alabama, and Thomas E. Kilby, the governor at the time the coin was issued; in the field are 22 stars, representing the total number of states of the Union at the time of Alabama's admission. The reverse shows an eagle with arrows on a shield.

Date	*Ex. Fine*	*Unc.*	*Amount Available*
1921	$27.50	$350.00	59,038
1921 with 2 ★ 2 in field on obverse	35.00	400.00	5,000

GRANT MEMORIAL

This half dollar was issued in 1922 to commemorate the 100th anniversary of the birth of Ulysses S. Grant. The coin was designed by Laura G. Fraser. The obverse shows a bust of Grant wearing a uniform; the reverse shows Grant's childhood home surrounded by trees. A star that appears on early issues of this coin is located on the obverse, to the right of the bust. This star seems to have no special significance.

Date	*Ex. Fine*	*Unc.*	*Amount Available*
1922 with star in field on obverse	$165.00	$625.00	4,256
1922	20.00	80.00	67,215

MONROE DOCTRINE CENTENNIAL

This half dollar was issued in 1923 to commemorate the 100th anniversary of the promulgation of the Monroe Doctrine. The coin was designed by Chester Beach. The obverse shows the busts of James Monroe and John Quincy Adams; the reverse shows the western hemisphere, portrayed by two female figures.

Date	*Ex. Fine*	*Unc.*	*Amount Available*
1923-S	$15.00	$60.00	274,077

HUGUENOT-WALLOON TERCENTENARY

This half dollar was issued in 1924 to commemorate the 300th anniversary of the settling of the Huguenots and the Walloons in the New World. The coin was designed by George T. Morgan. The obverse shows busts of Admiral Coligny and William the Silent; the reverse shows the ship *Nieu Nederland.*

Date	*Ex. Fine*	*Unc.*	*Amount Available*
1924	$15.00	$100.00	142,000

LEXINGTON-CONCORD SESQUICENTENNIAL

This half dollar was issued in 1925 to commemorate the 150th anniversary of the famous battles of the Revolutionary War. The coin was designed by Chester Beach. The obverse shows a statue of a Minuteman; the reverse shows the old Belfry at Lexington.

Date	*Ex. Fine*	*Unc.*	*Amount Available*
1925	$15.00	$70.00	160,013

STONE MOUNTAIN MEMORIAL

This half dollar was issued in 1925 to raise funds for the carving of Confederate leaders on Stone Mountain in Georgia. The coin was designed by Gutzon Borglum. The obverse shows General Lee and General "Stonewall" Jackson on horseback; the reverse shows a large eagle standing on a mountain crag.

Date	*Ex. Fine*	*Unc.*	*Amount Available*
1925	$8.50	$32.50	1,314,709

CALIFORNIA DIAMOND JUBILEE

This half dollar was issued in 1925 to commemorate the 75th anniversary of the admission of California to the Union. The coin was designed by Jo Mora. The obverse shows a miner panning for gold; the reverse shows a grizzly bear, the emblem of California.

Date	*Ex. Fine*	*Unc.*	*Amount Available*
1925-S	$20.00	$100.00	86,354

FORT VANCOUVER CENTENNIAL

This half dollar was issued in 1925 to raise funds to finance the celebration of the 100th anniversary of the building of Fort Vancouver. The coin was designed by Laura G. Fraser. The obverse shows a bust of Dr. John

McLoughlin, the builder of the fort; the reverse shows a frontiersman standing with a gun, and Fort Vancouver in the background.

Date	*Ex. Fine*	*Unc.*	*Amount Available*
1925-S	$85.00	$450.00	14,994

SESQUICENTENNIAL OF AMERICAN INDEPENDENCE

This half dollar was issued in 1926 to help raise funds for Fair held at Philadelphia to commemorate the 150th anniversary of the signing of the Declaration of Independence. The coin was designed by John R. Sinnock. The obverse shows busts of Presidents Washington and Coolidge; the reverse shows the Liberty Bell.

Date	*Ex. Fine*	*Unc.*	*Amount Available*
1926	$12.50	$60.00	141,120

OREGON TRAIL MEMORIAL

This half dollar originally was issued in 1926 in memory of the pioneers who crossed the Oregon Trail. The coin was designed by James E. Fraser and his wife, Laura G. Fraser. The obverse shows an Indian standing, with a map of the United States in the background; the reverse shows a covered wagon drawn by oxen.

Date	*Ex. Fine*	*Unc.*	*Amount Available*
1926	$ 8.50	$ 60.00	48,030
1926-S	8.50	60.00	86,354
1928	12.50	80.00	6,028
1933-D	20.00	140.00	5,008
1934-D	12.50	80.00	7,006
1936	10.00	70.00	10,006
1936-S	20.00	115.00	5,006
1937-D	12.50	70.00	12,008
1938			6,006
1938-D } set of three	—	220.00	6,005
1938-S			6,006
1939			3,004
1939-D } set of three	—	525.00	3,004
1939-S			3,005

VERMONT SESQUICENTENNIAL

This half dollar was issued in 1927 to commemorate the 150th anniversary of the Battle of Bennington and the Independence of Vermont. The coin was designed by Charles Keck. The obverse shows head of Ira Allen, the founder of Vermont; the reverse shows a Vermont catamount.

Date	*Ex. Fine*	*Unc.*	*Amount Available*
1927	$35.00	$160.00	28,108

HAWAIIAN SESQUICENTENNIAL

This half dollar was issued in 1928 to commemorate the 150th anniversary of the discovery of the Hawaiian Islands by Captain James Cook. The coin was designed by Chester Beach. The obverse shows bust of Captain Cook; the reverse shows a Hawaiian chief with a coconut tree and a village in background.

Date	*Ex. Fine*	*Unc.*	*Amount Available*
1928	$735.00	$1,800.00	10,008

MARYLAND TERCENTENARY

This half dollar was issued in 1934 to commemorate the 300th anniversary of the founding of the Maryland Colony by Lord Baltimore. Coin was designed by Hans Schuler. The obverse shows bust of Cecil Calvert (Lord Baltimore); the reverse shows the arms of Maryland.

Date	*Ex. Fine*	*Unc.*	*Amount Available*
1934	$25.00	$140.00	25,015

TEXAS CENTENNIAL

This half dollar was issued 1934–38 to commemorate the 100th anniversary of Texas's independence from Mexico in 1834. The coin was designed by Pompeo Coppini. The obverse shows a large eagle superimposed on a star. The reverse shows a winged Liberty kneeling, with her arms over a representation of the Alamo; a portrait of Sam Houston is at left and one of Stephen F. Austin is at right.

Date		*Ex. Fine*	*Unc.*	*Amount Available*
1935		$15.00	$ 70.00	61,350
1935				9,994
1935-D	set of three	——	210.00	10,007
1935-S				10,008
1936				8,911
1936-D	set of three	——	210.00	9,039
1936-S				9,064
1937				6,571
1937-D	set of three	——	210.00	6,605
1937-S				6,637
1938				3,780
1938-D	set of three	——	480.00	3,775
1938-S				3,816

DANIEL BOONE BICENTENNIAL

This half dollar was issued 1934–38 to commemorate

the 200th anniversary of Daniel Boone's birth in 1734. The coin was designed by Augustus Lukeman. The obverse shows bust of Daniel Boone; the reverse shows Chief Black Fish of the Shawnee Indians standing with Boone. In 1935, a small "1934" was added to the reverse.

Date		*Ex. Fine*	*Unc.*	*Amount Available*
1934		$10.00	$60.00	10,007
1935		8.50	60.00	10,010
1935-D		10.00	80.00	5,005
1935-S		10.00	80.00	5,005
1935 with small 1934		——	60.00	10,008
1935-D small 1934	pair	——	1,125.00	2,003
1935-S small 1934				2,004
1936	set of three	——	220.00	12,012
1936-D				5,005
1936-S				5,006
1937	set of three	——	525.00	9,810
1937-D				2,506
1937-S				2,100
1938	set of three	——	1,125.00	2,100
1938-D				2,100
1938-S				

CONNECTICUT TERCENTENARY

This half dollar was issued in 1935 to commemorate the 300th anniversary of the founding of the Connecticut colony. This coin was designed by Henry G. Kreiss. The obverse shows the Charter Oak. The reverse shows a large eagle.

Date	*Ex. Fine*	*Unc.*	*Amount Available*
1935	$37.50	$200.00	25,018

ARKANSAS CENTENNIAL

This half dollar was issued 1935–39 to commemorate the 100th anniversary of the admission of Arkansas into the Union in 1836. The coin was designed by Edward Everett Burr. The obverse shows the heads of an Indian and an American girl. The reverse shows a large eagle with spread wings.

Date		*Ex. Fine*	*Unc.*	*Amount Available*
1935	set of three	———	$160.00	13,012
1935-D				5,505
1935-S				5,506
1936	set of three	———	160.00	9,660
1936-D				9,660
1936-S				9,662

1937				5,505
1937-D	set of three	—	160.00	5,505
1937-S				5,506
1938				3,156
1938-D	set of three	—	330.00	3,155
1938-S				3,156
1939				2,104
1939-D	set of three	—	1,025.00	2,104
1939-S				2,105

HUDSON, NEW YORK SESQUICENTENNIAL

This half dollar was issued in 1935 to commemorate the 150th anniversary of the founding of the city of Hudson, New York. The coin was designed by Chester Beach. The obverse shows Henry Hudson's flagship *Half Moon*; the reverse shows Neptune on a whale, the seal of the city of Hudson.

Date	*Ex. Fine*	*Unc.*	*Amount Available*
1935	$160.00	$750.00	10,008

SAN DIEGO, CALIFORNIA-PACIFIC EXPOSITION

This half dollar was issued in 1935 and 1936 for the California-Pacific Exposition of 1935. The coin was designed by Robert Aitken. The obverse shows arms of the State of California; the reverse shows the observation tower and State of California Building at the exposition.

Date	*Ex. Fine*	*Unc.*	*Amount Available*
1935-S	$15.00	$65.00	70,132
1936-D	20.00	75.00	30,092

OLD SPANISH TRAIL

This half dollar was issued in 1935 to commemorate the 400th anniversary of the Cabeza de Vaca Expedition through the Gulf states. The coin was designed by L. W. Hoffecker. The obverse shows the head of a cow (the literal translation of the explorer's name is "head of a cow"); the reverse shows a yucca tree and a map of the Old Spanish Trail.

Date	*Ex. Fine*	*Unc.*	*Amount Available*
1935	$200.00	$825.00	10,008

RHODE ISLAND TERCENTENARY

This half dollar was issued in 1936 to commemorate the 300th anniversary of the founding of Providence, Rhode Island, by Roger Williams. The coin was designed by Arthur Graham Carey and John Howard Benson. The obverse shows an Indian welcoming Roger Williams at Slate Rock; the reverse shows the anchor of hope on a shield.

Date		*Ex. Fine*	*Unc.*	*Amount Available*
1936	set of three	——	$180.00	20,013
1936-D				15,010
1936-S				15,011

CLEVELAND GREAT LAKES EXPOSITION

This half dollar was issued in 1936 for the Great Lakes Exposition in commemoration of the 100th anniversary of the founding of Cleveland, Ohio. The coin was designed by Brenda Putman. The obverse shows a bust of Moses Cleveland (who planned the town); the reverse shows a map of the Great Lakes area with a compass pointed at Cleveland.

Date	*Ex. Fine*	*Unc.*	*Amount Available*
1936	$20.00	$60.00	50,030

WISCONSIN CENTENNIAL

This half dollar was issued in 1936 to commemorate the 100th anniversary of the founding of the Wisconsin Territory. The coin was designed by David Parsons and Benjamin Hawkins. The obverse shows a forearm holding a pickaxe over a mound of lead ore—the first Territorial Seal. The reverse shows a badger, the emblem of Wisconsin.

Date	*Ex. Fine*	*Unc.*	*Amount available*
1936	$32.50	$140.00	25,015

CINCINNATI MUSICAL CENTER

This half dollar was issued in 1936 to commemorate the 50th anniversary of Cincinnati as a center of music. The coin was designed by Constance Ortmayer. The obverse shows a bust of Stephen Foster; the reverse shows a draped figure of a woman playing a harp.

Date		*Ex. Fine*	*Unc.*	*Amount Available*
1936	set of three	——	$825.00	5,005
1936-D				5,005
1936-S				5,006

LONG ISLAND TERCENTENARY

This half dollar was issued in 1936 to commemorate the 300th anniversary of the settling of Long Island by Dutch colonists. The coin was designed by Howard Kenneth Weinman. The obverse shows heads of a Dutch pioneer and an Indian. The reverse shows a Dutch sailing vessel.

Date	*Ex. Fine*	*Unc.*	*Amount Available*
1936	$12.50	$50.00	81,773

YORK COUNTY, MAINE, CENTENNIAL

This half dollar was issued in 1936 to commemorate the 300th anniversary of the founding of York County, Maine. The coin was designed by Walter H. Rich. The obverse shows the seal of York County; the reverse shows a view of a stockade.

Date	*Ex. Fine*	*Unc.*	*Amount Available*
1936	$25.00	$130.00	25,015

BRIDGEPORT, CONNECTICUT, CENTENNIAL

This half dollar was issued in 1936 to commemorate the 100th anniversary of the incorporation of the city of Bridgeport, Connecticut. The coin was designed by Henry Kreiss. The obverse shows a bust of P. T. Barnum, a citizen of Bridgeport; the reverse shows a large eagle.

Date	*Ex. Fine*	*Unc.*	*Amount Available*
1936	$25.00	$115.00	25,015

LYNCHBURG, VIRGINIA, SESQUICENTENNIAL

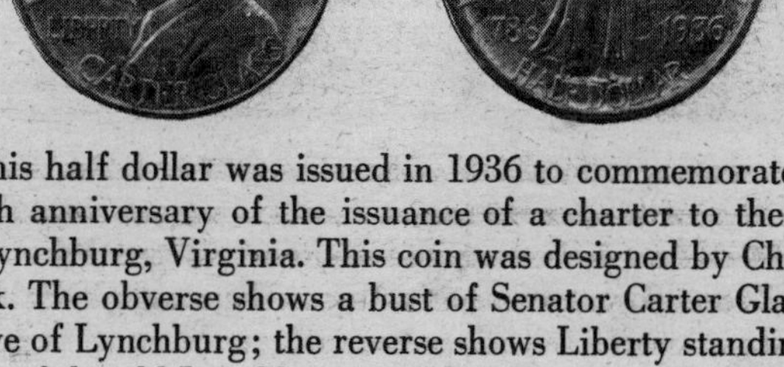

This half dollar was issued in 1936 to commemorate the 150th anniversary of the issuance of a charter to the city of Lynchburg, Virginia. This coin was designed by Charles Keck. The obverse shows a bust of Senator Carter Glass, a native of Lynchburg; the reverse shows Liberty standing in front of the old Lynchburg courthouse.

Date	*Ex. Fine*	*Unc.*	*Amount Available*
1936	$32.50	$140.00	20,013

ELGIN, ILLINOIS, CENTENNIAL

This half dollar was issued in 1936 to commemorate the 100th anniversary of the founding of the city of Elgin, Illinois. The coin was designed by Trygve A. Rovelstad. The obverse shows the head of a pioneer. The reverse shows the memorial statue of four pioneers that was erected on the anniversary.

Date	*Ex. Fine*	*Unc.*	*Amount Available*
1936	$32.50	$150.00	25,015

ALBANY, NEW YORK, CHARTER

This half dollar was issued in 1936 to commemorate the 250th anniversary of the issuance of a charter to the city of Albany, New York. The coin was designed by Gertrude K. Lathrop. The obverse shows a beaver gnawing on a maple branch; the reverse shows the standing figures of Governor Dongan, Mayor Schuyler, and Robert Livingston.

Date	*Ex. Fine*	*Unc.*	*Amount Available*
1936	$52.50	$230.00	16,887

SAN FRANCISCO-OAKLAND BAY BRIDGE

This half dollar was issued in 1936 to celebrate the opening of the San Francisco–Oakland Bay Bridge. This coin was designed by Jacques Schnier. The obverse shows a grizzly bear, the emblem of California; the reverse shows a view of the bridge.

Date	*Ex. Fine*	*Unc.*	*Amount Available*
1936	$20.00	$75.00	71,369

COLUMBIA, SOUTH CAROLINA, SESQUICENTENNIAL

This half dollar was issued in 1936 to commemorate the 150th anniversary of the founding of Columbia, South Carolina. The coin was designed by A. Wolfe Davidson. The obverse shows a figure of Justice standing between the old and the new state houses of South Carolina. The reverse shows a palmetto tree, the emblem of South Carolina.

Date		*Ex. Fine*	*Unc.*	*Amount Available*
1936				9,007
1936-D	set of three	———	$460.00	8,009
1936-S				8,007

ROBINSON-ARKANSAS CENTENNIAL

This half dollar was issued in 1936. This is the second coin commemorating the 100th anniversary of the admission of Arkansas to the Union (see *Arkansas Centenni-*

al, page 200). The new obverse, designed by Henry Kreiss, shows a bust of Senator Joseph T. Robinson.

Date	*Ex. Fine*	*Unc.*	*Amount Available*
1936	$25.00	$115.00	25,265

DELAWARE TERCENTENARY

This half dollar was issued in 1936 to commemorate the 300th anniversary of the landing of the Swedes in Delaware. The coin was designed by Carl L. Schmitz. The obverse shows the Swedish ship *Kalmar Nyckel;* the reverse shows the Old Swedes' Church at Wilmington, Delaware.

Date	*Ex. Fine*	*Unc.*	*Amount Available*
1936	$37.50	$160.00	25,015

BATTLE OF GETTYSBURG

This half dollar was issued in 1936 to commemorate the 75th anniversary of the Battle of Gettysburg (the 75th anniversary actually took place in 1938). The coin was designed by Frank Vittor. The obverse shows busts of a Union and a Confederate soldier; the reverse shows the shields of both armies with a double-bladed axe wrapped in fasces between them.

Date	*Ex. Fine*	*Unc.*	*Amount Available*
1936	$45.00	$140.00	26,928

NORFOLK, VIRGINIA, BICENTENNIAL

This half dollar was issued in 1936 to commemorate the 200th anniversary of the establishment of Norfolk from a township to a royal borough. The coin was designed by William Marks Simpson and Marjorie Emory Simpson. The obverse shows the seal of the city of Norfolk; the reverse shows the Royal Mace of Norfolk, which had been presented by Lieutenant Governor Dinwiddie in 1753.

Date	*Ex. Fine*	*Unc.*	*Amount Available*
1936	$45.00	$250.00	15,000

ROANOKE ISLAND, NORTH CAROLINA

This half dollar was issued in 1937 to commemorate the 350th anniversary of the founding of Sir Walter Raleigh's "Lost Colony" and the birth of Virginia Dare, the first white child born on the American continent. This coin was designed by William Marks Simpson. The obverse shows a bust of Sir Walter Raleigh; the reverse shows Elenore Dare carrying her infant daughter, Virginia.

Date	*Ex. Fine*	*Unc.*	*Amount Available*
1937	$20.00	$100.00	29,030

BATTLE OF ANTIETAM

This half dollar was issued in 1937 to commemorate the 75th anniversary of the Civil War battle for possession of Burnside Bridge. This coin was designed by William Marks Simpson. The obverse shows busts of Generals Lee and McClellan; the reverse shows Burnside Bridge.

Date	*Ex. Fine*	*Unc.*	*Amount Available*
1937	$75.00	$250.00	18,028

NEW ROCHELLE, NEW YORK

This half dollar was issued in 1938 to commemorate the 250th anniversary of the founding of New Rochelle by the Huguenots. The coin was designed by Gertrude K. Lathrop. The obverse shows John Pell with a calf; reverse shows a fleur-de-lis from the seal of New Rochelle.

Date	*Ex. Fine*	*Unc.*	*Amount Available*
1938	$60.00	$280.00	15,266

IOWA CENTENNIAL

This half dollar was issued in 1946 to commemorate the 100th anniversary of the admission of Iowa to the Union.

The coin was designed by Adam Pietz. The obverse shows the Iowa state seal; the reverse shows the first stone capitol building at Iowa City.

Date	*Ex. Fine*	*Unc.*	*Amount Available*
1946	$20.00	$70.00	100,057

BOOKER T. WASHINGTON MEMORIAL

This half dollar was issued 1946–51 to commemorate the 100th anniversary of the birth of Booker T. Washington. The coin was designed by Isaac Scott Hathaway. The obverse shows the head of Booker T. Washington; the reverse shows the memorial erected in his honor and his birthplace, a slave cabin.

Date		*Ex. Fine*	*Unc.*	*Amount Available*
1946				1,000,546
1946-D	set of three	——	$ 27.50	200,113
1946-S				500,279
1947				100,017
1947-D	set of three	——	45.00	100,017
1947-S				100,017
1948				8,005
1948-D	set of three	——	70.00	8,005
1948-S				8,005
1949				6,004
1949-D	set of three	——	140.00	6,004
1949-S				6,004

1950				6,004
1950-D	set of three	——	115.00	6,004
1950-S				512,091
1951				510,082
1951-D	set of three	——	80.00	7,004
1951-S				7,004

WASHINGTON-CARVER

This half dollar was issued 1951–54 in honor of Booker T. Washington and George Washington Carver. This coin was designed by Isaac Scott Hathaway. The obverse shows busts of Booker T. Washington and George W. Carver; the reverse shows a map of the United States.

Date		*Ex. Fine*	*Unc.*	*Amount Available*
1951				110,018
1951-D	set of three	——	$ 45.00	10,004
1951-S				10,004
1952				2,006,292
1952-D	set of three	——	60.00	8,006
1952-S				8,006
1953				8,003
1953-D	set of three	——	115.00	8,003
1953-S				108,020
1954				12,006
1954-D	set of three	——	45.00	12,006
1954-S				122,024

28

GOLD COMMEMORATIVE COINS

A total of nine different types of gold U. S. Commemorative coins have been issued. Of these, there are five one-dollar pieces, two quarter eagles and one fifty-dollar piece. The fifty-dollar piece has the highest face value of any official U. S. coin.

Coins in this section are listed in chronological order.

CONDITION (for all coins in this section): *Ex. Fine:* All details of design, lettering, and date sharp; coin should show only slight signs of circulation. *Unc.:* Coin should be in unused condition.

LOUISIANA PURCHASE EXPOSITION
(One Dollar)

Jefferson dollar *McKinley dollar*

These one-dollar pieces were issued in 1903 for the Louisiana Purchase Exposition held in 1904 in St. Louis to commemorate the 100th anniversary of the Louisiana Purchase. These coins were designed by Charles E. Barber and have two different obverses: one obverse shows the bust of Thomas Jefferson, who was president at the time Louisiana Territory was purchased from France; the second obverse shows a bust of President McKinley. The reverse, which bears inscriptions, is the same on both coins.

Date	*Ex. Fine*	*Unc.*	*Amount Available*
1903 Jefferson dollar ----	$225.00	$600.00	17,500
1903 McKinley dollar ----	225.00	600.00	17,500

LEWIS AND CLARK EXPOSITION
(One Dollar)

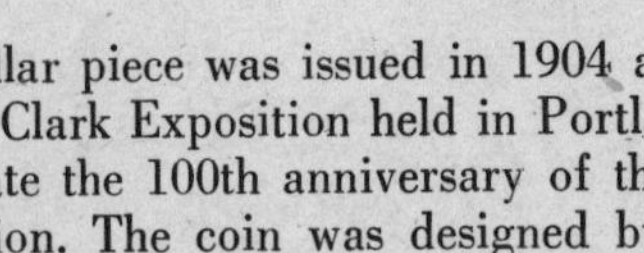

This one-dollar piece was issued in 1904 and 1905 for the Lewis and Clark Exposition held in Portland, Oregon, to commemorate the 100th anniversary of the Lewis and Clark Expedition. The coin was designed by Charles E. Barber. The obverse shows a bust of Meriwether Lewis; the reverse shows a bust of William Clark.

Date	*Ex. Fine*	*Unc.*	*Amount Available*
1904 ----------------------------	$500.00	$1,500.00	10,000
1905 ----------------------------	500.00	1,500.00	10,000

PANAMA-PACIFIC EXPOSITION
(One Dollar)

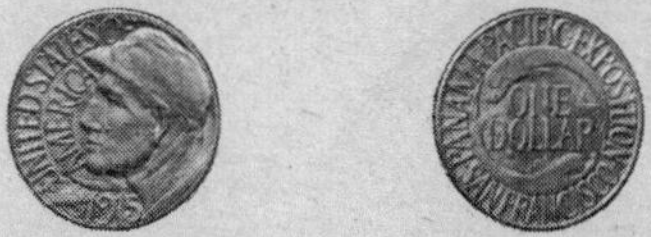

This one-dollar piece was issued in 1915 to commemorate the opening of the Panama Canal. This coin was designed by Charles Keck. The obverse shows head of man who portrays a Panama Canal workman wearing a cap; the reverse shows two dolphins encircling the value.

Date	*Ex. Fine*	*Unc.*	*Amount Available*
1915-S	$200.00	$600.00	25,000

PANAMA-PACIFIC EXPOSITION
(Quarter Eagle)

This quarter eagle ($2.50) was issued in 1915 to commemorate the opening of the Panama Canal. The coin was designed by Charles E. Barber and George T. Morgan. The obverse shows Columbia seated on a seahorse; the reverse shows an eagle with raised wings.

Date	*Ex. Fine*	*Unc.*	*Amount Available*
1915-S	$750.00	$1,750.00	6,750

PANAMA-PACIFIC EXPOSITION
(Fifty Dollars)

round

octagonal

These fifty-dollar pieces were issued in 1915 to commemorate the opening of the Panama Canal. These coins, designed by Robert Aitken, appear in two shapes, round and octagonal; both bear the same design. The obverse shows the head of Minerva wearing a helmet; the reverse shows an owl on a pine branch. The obverse and reverse of the octagonal coin show dolphins in the angles of the octagon.

Date	*Ex. Fine*	*Unc.*	*Amount Available*
1915-S round	——	$30,000.00	483
1915-S octagonal	——	22,500.00	646

McKINLEY MEMORIAL
(One Dollar)

This one-dollar piece was issued in 1916 and 1917 to help raise funds for a memorial building to be erected in Niles, Ohio, President McKinley's birthplace. The obverse, designed by Charles E. Barber, shows the bust of President McKinley; the reverse, designed by George T. Morgan, shows the memorial building to be erected.

Date	*Ex. Fine*	*Unc.*	*Amount Available*
1916	$200.00	$600.00	9,997
1917	250.00	700.00	10,004

GRANT MEMORIAL
(One Dollar)

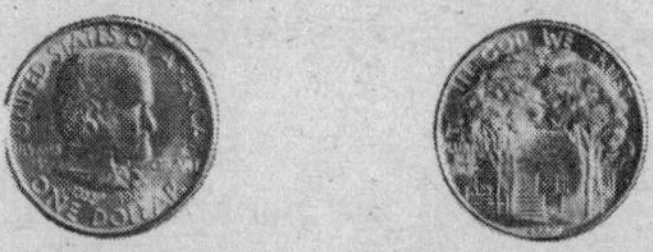

This one-dollar piece was issued in 1922 to commemorate the 100th anniversary of the birth of Ulysses S.

Grant. This coin, designed by Laura G. Fraser, shows the same design as the half-dollar silver counterpart. The obverse shows a bust of Grant; the reverse shows Grant's childhood home surrounded by trees. The same star that appears on the silver coin also appears on early issues of this coin.

Date	*Ex. Fine*	*Unc.*	*Amount Available*
1922 with star in field on obverse	$400.00	$1,150.00	5,016
1922	450.00	1,100.00	5,000

SESQUICENTENNIAL OF AMERICAN INDEPENDENCE

This quarter eagle ($2.50) was issued in 1926 to commemorate the 150th anniversary of the signing of the Declaration of Independence. This coin was designed by John R. Sinnock. The obverse shows Liberty standing holding torch of freedom and a scroll representing the Declaration of Independence. The reverse shows Independence Hall in Philadelphia.

Date	*Ex. Fine*	*Unc.*	*Amount Available*
1926	$250.00	$400.00	46,019

29

PRIVATE GOLD COINS

Private gold coins (known also as "pioneer" or "territorial" coins) were struck in the United States from about 1830 through 1861. Most private gold coinage originated in California; however, private issues were occasionally struck elsewhere—usually in areas where government coinage was scarce and gold was in abundance. Today, it seems incredible that privately owned banks, firms and families minted their own coinage; however, the shortage of official coins was acute and to conduct normal business, private issues were a near necessity. Private coinage provided a makeshift answer to the need for coins until the San Francisco Mint (opened in 1854) alleviated the problem.

Most privately-issued gold coins were eventually sent to U.S. Mints (and melted down for conversion into official coins); therefore, these private gold issues are rare today—and valuable.

On the following page are two examples of private U.S. gold coinage. It must be stressed, however, that most private issues had only three characteristics in common: 1) each coin bore the name or initials of the family or firm that minted it; 2) each coin bore the date of the year in which it was struck; 3) each coin bore the amount of its denomination. Consider the coins on page 224.

(1)

(2)

(1) This privately-issued $50 coin was struck in 1851. Look carefully to see the date at the bottom of the coin, its denomination (abbreviated "FIFTY DOLLS.") above the date, and the minter's name (Augustus Humbert) to the left of the date. (2) This privately-issued half eagle was struck in 1849. The date appears in the center of the coin; its denomination is at the bottom; the minter's initials (G.&N. for Sorris, Grieg & Norris) are above the date. It isn't possible to show all variations of private gold coinage; however, following is a partial list of men and companies who struck these coins and the areas in which they worked.

Templeton Reid (Ga.)
A. (or) C. Bechtler (N.C.)
Oregon Exchange Co. (Ore.)
Deseret (Utah)
Clark Gruber & Co. (Colo.)
John Parsons (Colo.)
G.W. Hall (Colo.)
Kellogg & Co. (Calif.)
Moffatt & Co. (Calif.)
Norris, Grieg & Norris—N.G. & N. (Calif.)
Augustus Humbert (Calif.)
Miners' Bank (Calif.)
F.D. Kohler (Calif.)
Dunbar & Co. (Calif.)
Baldwin & Co. (Calif.)
Wass, Molitor & Co. (Calif.)

If you find a gold coin with any of the above names on it, do *not* mail the coin to Stack's. Instead, write to Stack's, 123 West 57th St., New York, N.Y. 10019, describing the coin in detail. We will estimate the coin's worth (you can then mail it, insured adequately), and upon receiving and examining the coin, we will submit our firm offer to you.